TURN YOUR CUSTOMER ON:

23 Ways to Motivate Employees and Make Customers Love You

Kevin Billingsley
Brooke Billingsley

Copyright © 2007 by Perception Strategies, Inc.

All rights reserved. No part of this book shall be reproduced, stored in a retrieval system, or transmitted by any means, electronic, mechanical, photocopying, recording, or otherwise, without express written permission from the author. No patent liability is assumed with respect to the use of the information contained herein. Although every precaution has been taken in the preparation of this book, the author and publisher assume no responsibility for errors or omissions. Neither is any liability assumed for damages resulting from the use of information contained herein. For more information, address Literary Architects, 1427 W. 86th St., Ste 324, Indianapolis, IN 46260.

International Standard Book Number: 1-933669-02-0 (paperback edition)

International Standard Book Number: 1-933669-87-X (e-book edition)

Library of Congress Catalog Card Number: Available upon request.

Printed in the United States of America.

Note: This publication contains the opinions and ideas of its author. It is intended to provide helpful and informative material on the subject matter covered. It is sold with the understanding that the author and publisher are not engaged in rendering professional services in the book. If the reader requires personal assistance or advice, a competent professional should be consulted.

The author and publisher specifically disclaim any responsibility for any liability, loss, or risk, personal or otherwise, which is incurred as a consequence, directly or indirectly, of the use and application of any of the contents of this book.

For information on publicity, marketing, or selling this book, contact Bryan Gambrel, Marketing Director, Literary Architects, 317-462-6329. For information about becoming a Literary Architects author, contact Renee Wilmeth, Acquisitions Director, 317-925-7045. For information about working for Literary Architects, contact Tim Ryan, Publishing Director, 317-596-0049.

www.literaryarchitects.com

Cover design: GrafikNature

Copyediting: Kim Cofer

Interior design and composition: Amy Hassos

Proofreader: Julie Campbell

Indexer: Angie Bess

Dedication

To Ryan and Jordan

Acknowledgments

We would like to express our gratitude to God for blessing our business and bringing the right people into our lives. We would also like to thank Chuck and Lois Welling for the writing haven they provided in Florida; Lori Erickson Trump for her early editing of the book; Karen Ridenour for her inspiration and initial review of the book; our clients, especially Jim Tobalski, Mark Skaja, and Jean Kostelansky; Tim Ryan and the staff at Literary Architects for believing in the project; Mike and Laura Jaicomo for their friendship and constant cheerleading; Stefanie Kennebrew for holding down the fort; and Kevin's parents, Muriel and Jerry, for their lifelong support.

About the Authors

Kevin Billingsley is President of Perception Strategies, Inc., a consulting firm specializing in customer service assessment and training. His 25-year career included executive positions in the public sector, banking, and healthcare before founding Perception Strategies in 1998. His firm was the winner of the 2004 Blue Chip Business Award given to entrepreneurial firms who have faced obstacles and emerged stronger. He is a graduate of Michigan State University. Kevin can be reached at Kevin@perstrat.com.

Brooke Billingsley is a business entrepreneur and public speaker who engages audiences worldwide with her witty anecdotal style of "telling it like it is." Since 1999, she has been Vice President of Indianapolis-based Perception Strategies, Inc. Prior to that she served in the public sector for ten years as CEO of the Indiana Chapter of the Make-A-Wish Foundation® and CEO of the Indiana Chapter of ALS. Since 1978, Brooke has traveled throughout the world as a keynote speaker on topics including "Perception is Reality," the popular "Do You Have What it Takes to Deliver Great Customer Service?" and "It's All in the Way They See You!" Brooke can be reached at Brooke@perstrat.com.

Table of Contents

Dedication v
Acknowledgments v
About the Authors vi
Introduction xiii
    The Six Key Levels to Customer Service Excellence xvi
        1. Communicate a Never-Ending Commitment to Excellence ... xvii
        2. Hire People Who Want to Serve Others xviii
        3. Directly and Routinely Observe Employees in Action xviii
        4. Utilize Coaching Techniques xix
        5. Establish Accountability for Frontline Success xix
        6. Reward Those Who Excel in Customer Service xx
    The 23 Customer Turn Ons xxi

Chapter 1: Making It All about the Customer 1
    Customers Need to Feel the Love 2
    Best Buy 3
    Line of Sight 5
    The Freddie Story 6
    "I'm ready when you are." 7
    The "Just a Second" Rule 8
    "I'm done when you say I'm done." 9
    Car Dealership Banner 10
    Great Service Equals Job Security 11
    Tools 12
        Avoid Distractions 12
        Acknowledge Customers Immediately 12
        Recharge with Each Customer 13

Chapter 2: Relinquishing Power to the Customer 15
    The BMV 16
    "Determined to Delight" 19
    Counters and Glass Partitions 21
    Tie Goes to the Customer 22
    Tools 22
        Identify Opportunities to Show Abdication 22
        Look at the Big Picture 23
        Avoid Using Insider Terms 23

Chapter 3: No Rules 25
    Corporate Mandates 26
    Customers Are Perfectly Okay with Bending the Rules 27
    Estes Park Pizza 28
    Tools 29

Contents

Frontline Holds the Key 29
Apologizing 29
Assessing Rules 29

Chapter 4: Knowledgeable Employees 31
In a Perfect World, Every Employee Should Be Selling 31
Top 100 Hospital 33
"Because Word of Mouth Is Just Too Slow" 34
Tools 36
    Use Information Confidently 36
    Look for Selling/Cross-Selling Opportunities 36
    Provide Thorough Answers 36

Chapter 5: Employees Who Like to Serve 37
Your Customers Are on to You 37
Saboteurs, Inanimate Objects, and Attention Seekers 38
Hire People Who Want to Be Noticed 40
Message to New Hires 41
"If they make me do one more thing for customers, I'll quit!" 42
Employees Are More Aware of Their Shortcomings
    Than Managers Think 42
"Being a waiter in Europe is like being an attorney in the States." ... 43
Waves of Attitude 44
Tools 45
    Discover "Champions" 45

Chapter 6: Engaging the Customer 47
Abercrombie and Fitch 50
Scripts Are Not Engaging 51
Lowe's Again 51
Tools 53
    Engage Customers on Their Own Terms 53
    Show Enthusiasm 53
    Make Eye Contact 53
    Smile 53
    Hold Your Employees Accountable 54

Chapter 7: Employee Creativity 55
The Spa Lesson 55
Susan's Dive 56
Unique Service Shticks 57
Tools 59
    Use a Sense of Humor 59
    Encourage Creativity with Stipulations 59

Chapter 8: Teamwork 61
Showroom Teamwork 62
Guest Partners 63
Paradox: Most Employees Think They're Great! 64
The Obligatory Football Analogy 65
Tools 66
    Be Positive and Complimentary of Other Employees 66
    Don't Tolerate Negativism in Front of Customers 66
    Conduct Cross-Departmental Staff Meetings 67

Chapter 9: Respect 69
Home Depot Spray Paint 70
"O" Tickets 70
Friend of the Company 71
The Invisible Customer 73
Respecting Customers on the Telephone 74
Tools 75
    How to Handle "Stupid" Customers 75
    How to Manage Difficult Customers 76
    Learn from the Experience 76

Chapter 10: Friendliness 77
Customer Service Acting 101 78
Mandated Friendliness 79
Dental Desertion 81
"Hi," Staples Style 83
"Hi," Blockbuster Style 83
"Hi," Kinkos Style 84
Tools 85
    Create a Friendlier Culture 85
    Show Customers Little Kindnesses 85

Chapter 11: Matching the Customer's Pace 87
Acknowledgment Is Critical 88
Debit or Credit? 89
Don't Make Your Life Part of My Life, Please! 90
Tools 90
    Identify the Customer's Pace 90
    Develop a Process for Addressing Service Delays 91
    Explore More Effective Ways to Address Acknowledging the
    Customer Immediately 91

Chapter 12: Recognizing Customers 93
Do You Know Me? 94
Customers Aren't Strangers 94
The Ultimate Driving Machine 95

Dave Belanger 96
Why Not Use What You Know About Customers? 97
Tools 98
    Tips on Recognizing Customers 98

Chapter 13: Being Proactive 101
"Call to tell us you're coming." 101
Speaking Well of Other Employees 102
Olive Garden Survey 103
Keep the Customer 106
Tools 107
    Explain What You Are Going to Do for Customers 107
    Offer Names and Numbers 108
    Ask Questions 108

Chapter 14: Helping Customers Make Decisions 109
"They don't let us eat the food." 109
What Is the Difference between Selling and Customer Service? 110
Employee Identity Closes the Loop 111
Customer Service Selling 112
"All the doctors are good." 114
Darla's Fireworks 116
Tools 117
    Educate Employees on Product Knowledge 117
    Save Customers Time 118
    Customer Service Selling 118
    Recommend the Competition 119
    The Telephone Is a Sales Tool, Not a Necessary Evil 119

Chapter 15: Taking the High Road 121
Jumbo Man on the Jumbo Jet 121
When Customers Get Nasty 123
Explain to Diffuse, Not Light a Fuse 124
Customers Like Being "Handled" 124
Outside-In Perception Exercise 125
Apologizing Is an Effective Neutralizer 127
Tools 127
    Deter Employee Finger-Pointing 127
    Show Tolerance of Customers 128

Chapter 16: No Preconceived Notions 129
The Hospital Pillow 130
"Have you been with us before?" 131
Honda Dealership 132
Room and Board 134

Contents   ix

Tools 134
    Reading Customers 134
    Help Employees Identify and Discard Preconceived Notions 135

Chapter 17: Empowered Employees 137
  A Bread Shop Misses an Opportunity.. 138
  Applebee's 140
  Why Should Employees Care? 141
  Tools 142
    Build Trust in Your Employees 142
    Managers Need to Lead by Example 143

Chapter 18: Consistency 145
  The Mythical Origins of Bad Service 146
  The Pizza Hut Story 146
  What Happens to Employees When the Focus Is Put
    on Customers? 147
  Bennigan's 148
  "I have been after them for two months, and I am not giving up!" 149
  Customers Do Not Acknowledge Internal Boundaries.................. 150
  The Publix Lesson 151
  Every Customer Exchange Is a Separate One-Act Play.................. 152
  Tools 153
    "Your service may be monitored …" 153

Chapter 19: Responsiveness 155
  In Search of Swatches 157
  Greetings for Everyone 158
  Kinkos 160
  "Give Us a Call"—Take 1 161
  "Give Us a Call"—Take 2 162
  Pizza Nazi 162
  What If Every Job Depended on Tips? 163
  Responsiveness Is *Always* about People...................................... 165
  Tools 166
    Pay Closer Attention to Customers When Not Busy 166
    Managers Must Walk the Talk 167
    Treat Each Customer as an Opportunity 167

Chapter 20: Delivering on Promises 169
  "Magical Mission Statement".. 171
  "Please Don't Hug the Cashiers" 172
  "Treat People Better" 173
  "Customer Service" Desk.. 174

Why We Mystery Shop 175
Tools 176
    Mystery Shop organizational Claims 176
    Role-Play Promises 177
    Practice Scripted Slogans 177

Chapter 21: Follow Through 179
Arby's Guest Hotline 179
A Volunteer Gets a Letter 180
"Dismissing" Customers 181
High-Tech Store Receipts 182
Panera Bread 183
Tools 183
    Stay with Customers 183
    "What do you tell your spouse about work?" 184

Chapter 22: Employees Showing Pride in Their Work 185
Breckenridge SuperSlide™ 186
K-Mart 187
A Society of Ungracious Receivers 188
The Foundry Lesson 189
Tools 190
    "Act as if you own the place." 190
    Building an Awards Program 191

Chapter 23: Going the Extra Mile 195
R-E-P-E-A-T Performance 197
    Reinforce Behavior 198
    Educate 198
    Promote 198
    Expose 199
    Award 199
    Train Again 200
Rewarding "Extra Mile" Effort 200
Anatomy of an Incredible Call 201
Tools 204
    Implementing R-E-P-E-A-T Performance 204

Index 205

Introduction

Customer preferences are as varied as the stars in the skies, yet there are customer service strategies that, if performed by employees consistently and with the deliberate intent of pleasing the customer, will ensure that your customers have a positive and memorable experience with your organization. Ultimately, businesses that attract and retain customers best are those that will be profitable and successful.

On the surface, it seems like anyone could be taught to provide great customer service. How hard can it be for employees to simply deliver to customers the products and services your organization has to offer? Employees complicate what should be an intuitively simple process by failing to understand what motivates customers. Compound that with a genuine lack of desire to learn what it takes to meet customer needs, and customer service is stripped of the intuitive respect we must have for other human beings in order to deliver excellence. Out of necessity, we are forced to teach employees these values from scratch.

Our passion is customer service. While holding executive positions in the healthcare industry and the non-profit sector, we were directly involved in motivating and training employees to deliver excellent customer service. And we saw firsthand the positive effect that happy, repeat customers had on business. As owners of Perception Strategies, Inc., a consulting firm that specializes in customer service assessment and training, as well as mystery shopping, we have developed 23 techniques that we like to call customer *turn ons*. The term "turn on" is somewhat antiquated, taking us back to the psychedelic days of the 60s (minus the drugs of course), but we still find it appropriate simply because like psychedelia, it colorfully depicts customers leaving your organization enlightened, moved, respected, and ready to spread the joy of their positive experience.

What does your organization do to make customers happy? To turn them on? Make no mistake; there is a sizeable difference between satisfied and turned on. A customer who was satisfied with her latest hotel experience doesn't have any major complaints and, on her next trip, will consider returning to the same hotel. But a smile doesn't come to her face when she reminisces about the distracted front desk clerk or the bellman who took his time getting her bags to the room. The experience was just okay, perhaps even expected. But with so much going on in our lives, okay just isn't memorable, and it certainly isn't enough to build long-term customer loyalty.

In contrast, a turned on customer is a happy customer: she smiles when she thinks about your business. She recalls how the incredibly attentive front desk clerk made dinner reservations for her because the concierge was away from his desk, or the prompt and informative bellman who offered to set her up with a tour of the city. She tells her friends about the great experience she had with your business. Her friends tell their friends, and some of them become customers.

What was it that turned the customer on? A sincere smile, a volunteered effort, a well-timed question? Whatever it was, there was a connection between the customer and the employee that moved the experience to a new level. Often businesses do not train their employees to provide this level of service because it is mistakenly thought to be intuitive, or because it doesn't rely or depend on hard and fast rules like scripts or standards.

What if you could coach your employees to exhibit the characteristics that motivate customers to write glowing reviews on surveys and comment cards, that helps spread a positive message about your business, that builds customer loyalty? Did you ever sit down to figure out what those things are? We have. That's what this book is all about.

The summary reports we provide our clients contain the customer service trends we identified through a study of customer service processes and interactions with their employees. Additionally, Perception Strategies also maintains a database of employees and the types of extraordinary customer service they provide. We acknowledge these employees with our personal brand of recognition called Extra Mile Awards. By combining thousands of extraordinary efforts with a multitude of less than acceptable service trends, we have identified the 23 customer turn ons that are featured in this book.

We deal in service standards every day at Perception Strategies because they are the backbone of the service we provide. We evaluate employees on their adherence to specific actions they are expected to perform. Two of the most prominent actions are acknowledging customers immediately and greeting them with a warm smile. While extremely important to customers, these company expectations only become customer turn ons when they are taken to extremes, such as an employee who never stops smiling. Keep in mind, customers are thinking to themselves, "I will accept nothing less than you paying attention to me and smiling as if you care."

Let's assume we are conducting customer intercepts outside an upscale department store. Focusing on the immediate acknowledgment standard, we ask a customer if he recalls being acknowledged immediately by the cashier. The customer thinks and says, "Well, I don't remember her not noticing me, so I guess she probably did." Does that sound like a turned on customer? Of course if the cashier had been talking to another employee or fiddling with paperwork when the customer approached, the customer would have been irritated enough to remember the experience vividly, timing the encounter to the second.

So what would have to occur for the customer to give the researcher a turned on response? The employee might have fixed her eyes on the customer before the customer even approached (see Chapter 6, "Engaging the Customer"), smiled warmly, complimented the customer on something, addressed him by name based on the information in the system or on his credit card, offered a coupon for his next purchase, placed the item carefully in the bag, informed him that there is a special sale coming up, told him that he will be notified of the event, offered to place him on the e-mail or mailing list, walked out from behind the register, shaken the customer's hand, and thanked him for his business.

There are other actions the employee might have taken to leave a lasting impression, but the point is that a simple transaction has now become a memorable customer experience.

> At least 13 of the turn ons illustrated in this book were used in the previous example: Making it all about the customer, respect, relinquishing power to the customer, engaging the customer, creativity, delivering on promises, knowledge, friendliness, no preconceived notions, employees showing pride in their work, being proactive, recognizing customers, and going the extra mile.

During a presentation to a group of call center employees, Kevin asked the critical question, "Do you know what your customers like?" This talented and experienced group of customer service representatives remained silent. Finally, a solitary employee raised her hand and said, "No, but we know what pisses them off." To that we say, "It's not a turn on, but it's a start!"

The Six Key Levels to Customer Service Excellence

"Turn ons" are an outward reflection of your organization's customer service philosophy. This book will clearly identify for you the best ways to maximize customer perception through the positive actions of your employees.

However, in order to improve what the customer sees, hears, and feels, turn ons must be supported by a customer service infrastructure that is not seen by the customer. This infrastructure is much like *The Wizard of Oz* (Brooke's favorite movie). Although the Wizard sought to remain behind the scenes, he turned out to be the one who supported Dorothy, the Scarecrow, the Tin Man, and the Cowardly Lion by helping them see the qualities and abilities they already possessed.

So it is with your employees. They possess all the attributes necessary to turn on customers; they just need the support that will allow them to accept and flourish in this role. We call our infrastructure the Six Key

Levels to Customer Service Excellence. As each support level is added, the organization's resolve to exceed customer expectations is strengthened. All the turn ons discussed in this book are supported by one or more of the Six Key Levels.

The Six Key Levels are:

1. Communicate a Never-Ending Commitment to Excellence
2. Hire People Who Want to Serve Others
3. Directly and Routinely Observe Employees in Action
4. Utilize Coaching Techniques
5. Establish Accountability for Frontline Success
6. Reward Those Who Excel in Customer Service

1. Communicate a Never-Ending Commitment to Excellence

Create an attention-grabbing declaration that a *customer-first revolution* is vital to the success of the organization. This first level is intended to set the stage for change by communicating to all employees that management is firmly behind this push.

Make it clear to employees what the 23 Customer Turn Ons are, how this cultural change will be implemented, and what is expected of them.

To support this level, the organization must:

- Create organization-wide communication plans.
- Coordinate the development and dissemination of service standards.
- Conduct a customer service responsibility assessment.

2. Hire People Who Want to Serve Others

The first sign that the organization is willing to carry out a commitment to customer service excellence is the implementation of more selective hiring practices. For instance, do prospective employees like interacting with other people? Have they had success providing service in the past? Are they team players and do they understand what motivates consumers?

The organization must take steps to:

- Review and revise the interview process to assess an employee's customer service compatibility.
- Develop an employee customer service commitment document.
- Review and revise the customer service component for new employee orientations.
- Review and revise the employee evaluation process so that it supports customer service expectations.

3. Directly and Routinely Observe Employees in Action

Organizations sometimes assume their employees know how to achieve customer service excellence because when they were hired management told them what was expected of them. However, only through direct observation can one really understand how the organization is perceived, allowing managers to quickly address issues and make changes.

Direct observation is a two-fold process. First, we can think of no better way to effect change than to insert trained observants into the employee-customer relationship. That is why most, if not all, of the programs at Perception Strategies include a mystery shopping component. The other important observational effort must be to teach managers how to observe their employees and constantly coach them on what excellence looks like.

We recommend that organizations:

- Implement a mystery shopping program featuring real-time feedback, individual employee behaviors, and realistic scenarios.
- Conduct management training on the mystery shopping program focusing on utilization of the information and data.
- Train managers on the use of observational techniques.

4. Utilize Coaching Techniques

Leaders who discover the power of "listening to learn; asking to empower" create an exceptional organizational culture of employees who take greater ownership of their job. This is the essence of what is meant by corporate coaching. According to Dr. Craig Overmyer, Director of Coaching for The Canterbury Group, "Models such as RealTime Coaching, trademarked by Leadership Horizons, Inc., provide a 'do with' style of management that gets more done with and through others with less effort on the part of the leader."

A great coach develops employees to become leaders within their own realm of responsibility. Such leaders ask employees to follow through on their plans to further develop the skills, resources, and creativity to achieve their next level of personal best.

Employees who have a well-trained coach as a leader excel in productivity and in building customer loyalty beyond customer service. Leaders who are focused on merely "hearing to fix; telling to solve" tend to be the "do to" boss who barks out orders or a "do for" micromanager who ends up putting out fires and fixing problems over and over again. Without coaching as an essential dimension of leadership, corporations will be hard pressed to fully develop the human capital to the fullest.

5. Establish Accountability for Frontline Success

Customer service excellence is based on consistency and the faith that other employees will not drop the ball when it is passed to them. One missing link in the chain can irrevocably damage the prospect of a relationship, regardless of the strength of the other links. In time, the customer's perception of the service being delivered will most assuredly expose the lowest common denominator.

It is always preferable for the delivery of customer service to result in a long-term relationship, and yet the majority of customer service encounters are short stranger-to-stranger experiences. That is why consistency is so critical. The goal must be to do whatever is necessary to fortify all customer contact points with capable people so that there is never a "fall off."

The organization should:

- Develop a program to allow for cross-departmental feedback.
- Conduct a CUSTOMER FIRST management training program for all managers at the same time.
- Use high performers to train other employees.

6. Reward Those Who Excel in Customer Service

The ability to turn on a customer is primarily based on human interaction. Those who bring pleasure to customers should be recognized and rewarded above all other criteria.

The organization should:

- Use a comprehensive approach to recognition including customer comments, mystery shopping observations, and cross-departmental praise.
- Develop communication tools that highlight employee contributions to the new customer service culture.

The 23 Customer Turn Ons

Following is a list of the Customer Turn Ons discussed in this book; the numbers in parentheses indicate which of the Six Key Levels apply to each turn on.

1. Making It All About the Customer (1, 2, 3, 5)
2. Relinquishing Power to the Customer (1, 2, 3, 4, 5)
3. No Rules (1, 3, 5)
4. Knowledgeable Employees (1, 4)

5. Employees who Like to Serve (1, 2)
6. Engaging the Customer (2, 3, 4, 5)
7. Employee Creativity (2, 6)
8. Teamwork (1, 2, 3)
9. Respect (1, 2, 3)
10. Friendliness (2, 5)
11. Matching the Customer's Pace (3, 4, 5)
12. Recognizing Customers (1, 4)
13. Being Proactive (2, 3, 4, 5)
14. Helping Customers Make Decisions (3, 5)
15. Taking the High Road (1, 3, 4)
16. No Preconceived Notions (1, 2, 3, 4, 5, 6)
17. Empowered Employees (1, 5)
18. Consistency (1, 3, 4, 5)
19. Responsiveness (1, 2, 3)
20. Delivering on Promises (1, 2, 3)
21. Following Through (4, 5)
22. Employees Showing Pride in Their Work (1, 2, 5)
23. Going the Extra Mile (1, 2, 3, 4, 5, 6)

There is no magical customer service initiative that will suddenly and permanently alter the course your organization is on. Getting your employees to uniformly see the light is hard work; it requires the proper infrastructure and dedication from every level of the organization. We believe that if you adopt and follow the lessons and tools conveyed with the following 23 Turn Ons, you will have all the ammunition you need to motivate employees to see their roles in a new light, consistently provide excellent customer service, and as a result, begin turning your customers on!

Chapter 1
Making It All about the Customer

> "Great customer service necessitates that employees acquire tunnel vision for the benefit of the customer."
>
> —Kevin and Brooke Billingsley

Key Levels to support the turn on:
1. Communicate a Never-Ending Commitment to Excellence
2. Hire People Who Want to Serve Others
3. Directly and Routinely Observe Employees in Action
5. Establish Accountability for Frontline Success

The act of providing customer service is nothing more than suspended reality. It's a game but with very real consequences. The ground rules for the game are that customers intuitively know that you, the service provider, don't know them from a hole in the ground but still have the responsibility of serving them in a friendly manner. They know that this is all you do all day long, and they also know it is ultimately your job to sell them something. But during the course of the game, points are deducted from the employee for taking this knowledge for granted. Instead, to actually win the game, the employee must treat the customer like a friend; enthusiastically, yet gently, guiding the customer to a mutually beneficial decision or experience.

"Go ahead," the customer challenges, "Make it all about me. I may not expect it, and I may not even think I deserve it, but I sure do want it." With every second of every encounter, customers must be made to feel that they are all that matters. The *turn on* for customers is that a stranger has seemingly made it her goal in life to myopically focus on their needs. It is an emotional high to perceive that another human being cares that much about you. It makes people feel special.

Given that most customer service encounters last only seconds, and sometimes minutes, customers don't worry that the attention they are receiving may not be entirely genuine. There is one caveat: Customers are okay with employees faking it, as long as employees don't make it obvious that they're faking it.

Great customer service is completely non-discriminatory. Every customer should be treated the way he or she wants to be treated. The challenge for employees is to discover what that is. Some organizations shy away from the challenge because it turns out to be more difficult than they ever imagined. They don't "have the stomach for it" and suffer the consequences.

Customers Need to Feel the Love

Have you ever been in a situation where you are next in line to be assisted, and the employee behind the counter is talking on the phone? Kevin had this experience while conducting a mystery shop of a billing department. He noticed the employee was smiling and laughing and he began to smile himself. He excused the fact that she was not helping him because he hoped to be a recipient of all that goodwill when she hung up. No such luck. She got off the phone and greeted him with a stone cold look that quickly chilled him. Before he had time to give it some rational thought, he believed that perhaps he was somehow responsible for ending her fun.

Suddenly, it hits him. It's not personal. It isn't that she dislikes him—she dislikes all customers.

To be honest, for a brief instant, situations like this hurt. As customers, we know we deserve better, not just because we are the customer and we're "paying for her job," but because we can't believe another human being would treat us so badly. A stranger on the street could muster up more caring.

If your organization is oblivious to this type of employee behavior, or worse yet, excuses it, it is time to make your employees aware of how they are being perceived. A form of direct observation, either by the manager or through mystery shopping, can lay the groundwork for coaching and improved behavior.

Best Buy

Kevin and our oldest son Ryan spent 15 minutes in the computer area of a Best Buy watching employees fly by. Finally an energetic young man said, "Is there a *quick* question I can answer?" Wondering if anyone gets to ask lengthy questions, Kevin said, "If you consider buying a computer a quick thing." The employee caught Kevin's drift and remained with them, giving a cursory explanation of their offerings. Kevin then asked him for the specifications of a computer that was missing the small sign that displayed the specs. He fumbled through the notebook he was carrying, convinced he had the information. Reaching the end of the book, he mumbled an apology and instead produced a photo of his girlfriend and proudly proclaimed, "Isn't she a babe!" Kevin and Ryan gawked at each other in amazement. He clearly lost sight of the need of the customer and substituted it with getting more personal than Kevin and Ryan were comfortable with. They intentionally didn't buy a computer from him.

When Kevin experienced sub-par service at several Best Buy store locations, he asked an employee if he had received customer service training. To reassure him, the employee indicated that it was not really necessary in his case because he had been in the Navy and also had driven a truck for Coca Cola. What?!

To get a sense of the culture that fostered this kind of customer service, Kevin met with the store manager. He anticipated that the manager would exhibit the same poor customer service he experienced from the frontline employees. However, to his great surprise, the opposite was true. She actually talked a good game and seemed to have a grasp of what was needed to provide good service. She succinctly summarized her philosophy by saying "I want them to laugh and have fun." Kevin found this pro-employee approach admirable, but the next step is to ask, "What about the customer? Is your goal to make it fun for them too? Can we all share in the fun, or are consumers like children on a playground where you point to the sandbox and say, 'Go play'"?

Clearly, a disconnect existed. The store manager was educated on a corporate culture that encouraged employees to have fun. And it was clear from the company's advertising campaign that its marketing strategy was designed to encourage the consumer to have fun in the store as well. But for all the good intentions and millions of dollars spent in advertising to promote a "fun" environment, none of it translated to the employees working on the floor, and through them to the customer.

Perhaps the manager was attempting to execute this particular strategy, but it was completely invisible to the consumer. She was in denial about the reality of the situation; that is to say, the consumer's perception. For all her good customer service talk, Best Buy's telephone still rang 50 times with customer complaints, eye contact between employee and customer was a rarity, and thank-you's were non-existent.

Kevin retold this story once during a presentation to a senior management group. The CEO challenged Kevin by saying that "that is not what Best Buy is about." He never explained himself, but Kevin believes he was convinced that the superstore was all about low prices, and because of that one should not expect great customer service. Could it be that the CEO felt that a company that sells goods directly to consumers with a sales staff on the floor is not in the customer service business? Kevin could only imagine that this CEO was one of those rare consumers who does not want assistance, and for him the strategy worked just fine.

But the question remains: What service provider can afford to declare that excellent customer service is outside their realm of responsibility? Even if the company were to execute its internal and external strategies flawlessly, negative consumer perception would keep the company from reaching its full potential.

Unfortunately, Best Buy failed to think about what the majority of its customers expected, and failed to see the business from their perspective. They thought they could dictate the terms of the experience without regard for customer perception. While you can have a low-price strategy, you cannot ignore the fact that business can be won or lost by the frontline employees on the showroom floor.

The first test for any truly customer-centered culture is to commit the organization to think "customer first" in everything they do. We run into example after example of broken promises and customer service initiatives gone sour. Nearly every organization steps up to the customer service excellence starting line at one time or another, but few stay in the race. What happens in the interim is that the customer service champion is sidetracked, priorities are realigned, and gaps in execution grow wider.

Line of Sight

Kevin walked into a coffee shop one evening. He walked up to the register to order a cup of coffee. In front of him, a manager was busily filling out paperwork. Even if the manager was totally engrossed in his work, he had to have known Kevin was there. After approximately a minute of no acknowledgment, the manager looked up and asked if he could help. The manager had decided when the service would occur, not Kevin. It always disappoints customers when they are put on the employee's time frame rather than their own.

Our own personal rule—one that we always pass on to clients—is that if you are in the customer's line of sight, you are fair game for criticism. When customers are ready for service, they don't really care what the manager is doing or how important that work is to him. In fact in this situation, most customers don't care if the manager has a deadline to get vital information to corporate headquarters within the next 30 seconds.

The fact that it was a manager failing to make it all about the customer is even more disturbing. It sets a poor example for frontline employees. It's our guess that the next time an employee at this coffee shop is asked to do something like inventory, they are likely do it in front of customers, because their manager did it.

What should this manager have done? The first thing would be to not do paperwork at the service counter. Although a little less acceptable, he could have given eye contact, smiled, and indicated with one finger raised—the "just a second" rule, which is discussed in more detail later in the chapter—that he would be with Kevin shortly. That tells customers he will be with them as soon as he is done. Would most customers accept that? Sure they would.

Even if the customer has a good guess as to what the manager is working on, the manager is not free to *presume* that the customer understands. Employees must never take customers for granted. The rule is for employees to never presume anything with customers, and never try to make them empathize with activities unrelated to the customer.

The Freddie Story

Sometimes organizations have considerations other than an individual's readiness to provide excellent customer service when placing that person in a frontline position. One such example is helping to mainstream disadvantaged people into the workforce when they are not yet ready. As sensitive a subject as this is, it is unfortunate that, in some cases, this is done without realizing the impact it may have on customer service. On a grocery-shopping trip to a Meijer Supermarket store, we were assisted by a cashier we will call Freddie. It was immediately apparent that Freddie was facially disfigured and perhaps self-conscious about it. When Brooke attempted to talk to him, she received no response. In fact, throughout the transaction, Freddie never said a word.

When it came time to weigh vegetables, Freddie became frustrated with his inability to work the register. Brooke tried to assist him but his frustration only intensified. He finally just rang the bulk items through for a penny. After the completed transaction, which took twice as long as those around us, Freddie said nothing. Brooke immediately sought a manager.

She questioned the young manager about why the store would cause an employee so much stress by placing him in a position he had not been properly trained for and, in the process, subject their customers to such poor service. The manager retorted that Freddie had a disability, inferring that it was Brooke's problem because she was being insensitive to Freddie's handicap. Brooke made it clear to the manager that her concern was not with Freddie, but with a store that set him up to fail.

Companies should always consider the ramifications of their actions on the customer when they opt to make staffing changes, even if those changes are altruistic. At their own peril, Meijer can choose to lower their service standards, but they don't have the power to arbitrarily lower customer expectations. Perhaps Freddie would have responded with something other than fear if the store had prepared him better. Instead, they pointed to his disability as the reason for the poor outcome, rather than their poor training.

"I'm ready when you are."

If employees could embrace one simple mantra before entering into each encounter with a customer, they would prevent most of the occurrences that ultimately lead to negative perceptions from customers. That mantra is "I'm ready when you are."

This simple philosophy implies that the employee is immediately accessible to the customer. Actually, it indicates even more. It suggests that the employee is ready *before* the customer is. This respect for the customer—this willingness to make it all about the customer— pre-empts animosity that can occur before anyone has even spoken. Even a few seconds ticking off on the clock can have a dramatic effect on a customer's disposition. If an employee is in full view and customers are forced to wait even five seconds, some will get frustrated; after 10 seconds they are angry; and after 20 seconds, they may want to hurt someone. Every second that a customer has to wait jeopardizes the customer relationship.

Our firm, Perception Strategies, conducts a customer service training exercise in which attendees simulate how it appears when an employee ignores the person in front of them because they are busy focusing on something else. Attendees then demonstrate how it appears when an employee is looking at the customer before the customer is even ready. The intent is to show how effortless an encounter can be when the employee is waiting on the customer rather than the other way around. Attendees can *feel* the length of time firsthand. As an employee, 20 seconds may feel like nothing, but when the roles are reversed, attendees acting as customers discover that 20 seconds is an uncomfortable amount of time.

Combined with a smile, we contend that very little can go wrong when employees adopt the mantra of "I'm ready when you are." The employee is positioned to succeed. This is an open invitation to join into a relationship; therefore, it is important for employees to practice giving customers immediate attention and determine if some process changes are in order to make this happen.

The "Just a Second" Rule

Sometimes the simplest things can make the biggest difference in customer service. Employees often miss the opportunity to diffuse the critical seconds between initial contact and acknowledgment by signifying "I'll be with you in a second." Even when it is *not* obvious to a customer that the employee is engaged, it is still extremely important for employees to make every effort to acknowledge the customer's presence.

The "just a second" rule is a simple gesture that should be used when an employee is already working with someone or is on the telephone. By quickly holding up the index finger to acknowledge the customer, the employee has diffused the inevitable frustration that comes with being seen but not served by them.

"I'm done when you say I'm done."

If the opening mantra "I'm ready when you are" signifies the attitude with which every encounter should begin, the closing mantra "I'm done when you say I'm done" promises a never-ending commitment to the customer. It implies that employees will take whatever time and effort is necessary to satisfy the customer. Also, it displaces the impression of a time limit or that there are more pressing matters the employee must attend to.

Imagine the opportunities that would exist if every employee were to approach his or her job with this attitude. While most customers will not choose to take advantage of an open invitation to extend the encounter, it nonetheless remains symbolic of not trying to hustle the customer along.

What if customers take employees up on this "offer without an end"? The result would likely be more sales. Sending the message that "I am here as long as you need me" may spark some additional creativity on the customer's part, such as, "You know, I was really hoping to find a shirt to go with these pants. Do you think you could help me?" This approach never stops exceeding the customer's expectations; in turn, it leads to storytelling, word-of-mouth marketing, and a clear competitive advantage over those unwilling to make the offer.

Most managers consider this approach unproductive and see it as unnecessarily bending over backwards for customers. At what cost? The manager of facilities for a large Midwestern hospital once explained to Brooke that his housekeeping people would never be recognized for exceptional service because it was unproductive for them to take twenty minutes to personally escort someone to their destination. She shared with the manager that his employees actually have four possible choices when faced with someone in need of directions: They can ignore the customer, resulting in a shockingly negative outcome; they can unintentionally give poor directions, causing a frustratingly negative outcome; they can give accurate directions, which will be perceived as positive-yet-unmemorable; or they can escort the customer to the destination and achieve an unexpectedly positive outcome.

The concept of productivity that many managers hold dear is inherently anti-customer. If an employee doles out time in small increments in an effort to be fair and consistent for all customers, *every* customer gets shortchanged. Customers aren't thinking to themselves, "Well at least the person in front of me didn't get one more second than I did!" Customers are willing to wait a little longer if they know that their experience is going to be as complete as everyone else's.

"I'm done when you say I'm done" is a simple way to remind employees that they must be open to anything and to learn to go with the customer's flow. Phrases such as "Can I get you anything else?" and "Is there anything else I can do for you?" allow for the last word to be the customer's. Offers like "Can I send that to you?" or "Would you like me to have someone call you?" make it all about the customer, creating opportunities for extraordinary service and future sales.

Car Dealership Banner

When Kevin walked into the service staging area of the BMW dealership to check on the status of his car, he noticed for the first time a very large banner hanging from the ceiling that encouraged customers to give the service department high marks on the survey instrument they were using. Usually, signs of this nature disguise their pleading by including the phrase "*if* you are satisfied" or "tell us what we need to do to get a five." Not this sign. Kevin felt like he was being ordered to be satisfied or else. Fortunately, his experience was exceptional and he was able to share that when the telephone surveyor called.

The banner represents a classic example of making it about the company, not the customer. The majority of customers who really thought about the banner would probably deduce that pressure from BMW corporate is causing the dealership to strong-arm its customers. However, is any customer compliant enough to provide feedback just to help inflate satisfaction scores? To what end? Is it going to make future experiences better?

Even if some customers heed the call and do as the dealership asks, the data merely creates a false sense of security. It may get corporate off the dealership's back, but it does nothing to turn the customer on. And because satisfaction scores can't change employee behavior, employees are rewarded for doing nothing differently.

Making it about the customer means never suggesting what the customer can do to help out the organization. Let your excellent customer service speak for itself, and allow the unfettered feedback of your customers show you the way to behavioral change and excellence.

Great Service Equals Job Security

One of our clients complained that his employees' behavior was not improving, even though their business was being seriously threatened by the competition.

We asked the client if his staff was aware that their jobs were also being threatened. Surprisingly, he said the company had never delivered that message, but he thought it would be a good idea. We do too.

Employees are often oblivious to the fact that exceptional customer service can equal job security. As Forler Massnick wrote in *The Customer is CEO*, "There is logic to putting the customer first. Criminal investigators talk of following the money trail. Well, the money trail starts with the customer. No customer, no money; no money, no company. Anyone and everyone can understand that. What is not so easily understood is how everything else falls into line once customers are granted their rightful place."

At the beginning of this chapter, we described customer service as an unreal game with very real outcomes. The reality is that lost points represent lost customers. Lost customers mean lost jobs. The message to employees must be to play the game but play it for keeps.

Tools

Avoid Distractions

Telephones, other employees, and other customers must all be considered secondary to focusing on the customer in front of you. When employees are confronted with distractions, or they are involved in another activity when a customer engages them, they must use the following tactics to address the situation:
- Quickly but politely let the distracter know you will be with them as soon as you finish with the current customer.
- Always try to give an estimation of when you will be with them.
- Use the "just a second" rule if you are unable to speak to the distracter.
- When appropriate, apologize to the customer for interruptions.

Acknowledge Customers Immediately

Nothing is more important in a customer-employee encounter than the first few seconds when the customer chooses to engage an employee. Acknowledging customers is perhaps the most important customer service behavior because it serves as the starting point for every encounter.
- Train employees on the "I'm ready when you are" approach to pre-emptive acknowledgment.
- Conduct role-playing exercises on the proper way to acknowledge customers.
- Coach employees by videotaping their customer greetings.
- Implement a "zero time" policy for acknowledging customers.

- Reward employees for achieving a perfect score for the acknowledgment service standard.

Recharge with Each Customer

Creating freshness with the singular focus of satisfying the next new customer is the only way to achieve service excellence. Employees must make each customer experience fresh because they are encountering a new customer every time. Imagine focusing on each customer in complete isolation. For those of you old enough to remember, visualize the *Get Smart* "Cone of Silence."

Chapter 2
Relinquishing Power to the Customer

> "Perhaps the most central characteristic of authentic leadership is the relinquishing of the impulse to dominate others."
>
> —David Cooper

Key Levels needed to support the turn on:

1. Communicate a Never-Ending Commitment to Excellence
2. Hire People Who Want to Serve Others
3. Directly and Routinely Observe Employees in Action
4. Utilize Coaching Techniques
5. Establish Accountability for Frontline Success

Given how incredibly unpredictable, illogical, and unknowledgeable some customers can be, relinquishing power to them may sound a little crazy. Everyone knows customers aren't really qualified to be "the boss," so why pretend? Right?

The obvious answer is that customers respond much better to a healthy imbalance between customer and employee, one that is lopsided in the customer's favor. Customers are not turned on by employees who treat them as unimportant or somehow inferior.

In the broadest sense, relinquishing power to customers simply means thinking "customer first." But more specific to this chapter, it means granting customers the leading role in your organization even though they may be less knowledgeable than your employees about products or services. It means "giving it up for the customer" even if your organization is the only place they can receive a particular service. Schools and government agencies immediately come to mind, but there are certainly other organizations and institutions that can't imagine why in the world they would want to "turn on" a customer.

At the heart of the 23 Customer Turn Ons is the recognition that organizations become successful by building customer loyalty; and the thing that customers want most is to be treated with respect and enthusiasm. Some organizations might argue that they don't have customers. It's tempting to think that policemen only serve the law and that teachers only serve education, but doesn't the old cliché "I pay his salary" still apply? For instance, if you were to go to a high school to talk to a guidance counselor about your child, wouldn't you technically be a customer? With that would come the expectation that you would be greeted promptly and courteously, that you would be treated like an adult and not another child, and that you would be thanked for taking the time to meet. Service, regardless of the circumstances, should have the same turn ons apply.

Relinquishing power to customers is considered a turn on in these situations because it is often unexpected. Aren't we all incredibly grateful when we talk to an extremely pleasant person at a government agency? The call may have been something you were dreading because you envisioned a web of transfers and unanswered questions, but instead, you got someone who quickly, respectfully, and pleasantly handled your transaction.

Think about your organization's interactions with the people you deal with on a regular basis. Do you provide a service where your employees don't see the need to turn on customers? The challenge is to use the 23 Customer Turn Ons to train them to abdicate a little of their "power" to make the experience more pleasant for customers.

The BMV

Kevin was approaching a birthday and was required to renew his driver's license. Brooke decided to get hers out of the way as well. We like airports because they are great places to people-watch, but airports, or malls for that matter, have nothing on the BMV. It is truly the great melting pot: People of all ages and races are crammed together, and stand on equal footing, as they wait to be served by the state bureaucracy. When we arrived that day, the line was out the door.

The license branch of the Bureau of Motor Vehicles is such an easy target for customer service horror stories that it has become somewhat clichéd—perfect fodder for stand-up comedians. Given that serving customers is all they do, one would think they would be experts. We have to admit we were naïve enough to think that things just might be different. Surely by now they have advanced to 1990 technology? Isn't this the age of data and information? Isn't the BMV in the data and information business? Instead, they line us up like cattle, call our number, and then demand that *we* get everything right or they will send us on our way. Smiles and eye contact, at least at our branch, are optional and rare.

On this particular visit, we were standing in line just inside the doorway. This gave us an excellent vantage point to observe the innocent souls checking in and those thankfully departing. Customer after customer walked by us shaking their heads in utter disbelief as if to say, "That's two hours of my life I'm never getting back!"

Once past the bilingual traffic cop, we sat down for a different view of the show. One elderly woman who must have been nearly 90 years old was offered a chair in the aisle. Almost instantly from the other side of the counter came a reprimand from a young man who instructed the woman that she couldn't sit there. With a rare shot of defiance, a disobedient taxpayer leaned over and told the woman to "ignore the punk."

When we were called up to renew our driver's licenses, we noticed a wire basket strategically placed in the center of the long counter. Inside it were forms for the STAR AWARD, which acknowledges employee good deeds, such as handling a difficult situation, doing something special for a fellow employee, providing outstanding customer service, and the like. Below the customer feedback portion was a box called the STAR COUPON, which was obviously intended to go to the person acknowledged.

This sounds like a good idea, right? And it probably was a long time ago. But this unattractive, single-sheet form was clearly a reprint of a reprint of a reprint. The revision date in the upper right-hand corner was 7/19/94! This pathetic looking award form has been sitting there for more than a decade. As a BMV employee, I'm sure getting one of these would certainly make his or her whole year! It's time to revise.

Lest you think we are picking on the BMV over an employee acknowledgment form, the issue is really about the execution of a program that was originally intended to accomplish something. More than twelve years ago someone, perhaps a well-intentioned manager, had an idea to give employees an "atta-boy." But now, that vision is collecting dust in a wire basket, and it is possibly doing more harm than good.

Larry Bossidy and Ram Charan write in *Execution—The Discipline of Getting Things Done*, "Without execution, the breakthrough thinking breaks down, learning adds no value, people don't meet their stretch goals, and the revolution stops dead in its tracks. What you get is change for the worse, because failure drains the energy from your organization." The germ of an idea that was this award is now pointless and, as Bossidy and Charan put it, any momentum and goodwill it generated sputtered to a halt long ago.

There must have been a time when the BMV asked its employees to reach out and encourage customer involvement. But now, the STAR AWARD sits dormant. There is absolutely no justification for the award's existence, given the dismal state of customer service at the BMV. No employees are showing up for work with the goal of getting a STAR AWARD. There is no effort to direct customers to the award. There is absolutely no connection between behavior and the intent of the award. As a result, it becomes a joke perpetrated on the state's taxpayers. Not surprisingly, nowhere in the license branch is there a form that allows you to suggest improvements.

The branch office we frequent most often was recently relocated to a strip mall about a half a mile from the old branch. The outcome was a larger room; same employees. They even managed to make the room starker and less inviting. Needless to say, the move was not predicated on customer satisfaction or comfort. One more chance to improve the customer's experience is denied.

What might a positive experience at the BMV be like? If we must be there for an hour or two, it would be nice if the BMV was a warmer and more inviting place to visit. But seeking the advice of interior design and traffic flow experts to create a more pleasant environment is probably budgetarily out of the question. A turn on at the BMV would involve hiring pleasant people trained in customer service basics, who consistently greeted visitors with a smile and a "What can I do for you today?"

When there is no alternative, customers resolve to endure the situation and simply hope the end will come soon. The BMV is hardly the only example of an institution that seems reluctant to relinquish power to customers. Based on the many studies we have conducted in healthcare, we find that patients in hospitals feel much the same way. They are a captive audience where someone else is calling the shots, even though they are paying the bills. When customers are in that situation, they rationalize that it is best to just keep quiet out of fear that service may actually get worse. This is especially true for seniors.

"Determined to Delight"

Kevin helped to create a customer service initiative called "Determined to Delight" at a hospital he worked for several years ago. Determined to Delight was a management "rounds" program where each manager was responsible for visiting the newly admitted patients in the hospital. Every member of the management staff, including senior management, was assigned a different day. The goal was threefold: to put managers in direct contact with customers (especially those managers who rarely had the opportunity), discover if the patients had any issues regarding the level of service being provided, and show that the people who ran the hospital really did care about the patients.

As Kevin was conducting his rounds, a senior nurse stopped him on her unit and asked him what he was doing. Her curiosity suggested that she was wondering why management-types were invading her turf. Kevin explained the merits of the program to her and talked about the push to improve customer service. After hearing his explanation, she said with conviction, "You know, if patients would learn to be nice to me, I'd be nice to them."

The thought, "I hope there aren't more of you out there!" crossed Kevin's mind. This nurse didn't get her viewpoint overnight, and Kevin knew better than to assume that she was alone in her outlook.

In fact, this sentiment was brought into new light around the same time Kevin was conducting focus groups of both employees and former patients to get their perspectives on service and patient care. In the middle of a patient session, a young woman who had delivered a baby in the hospital said very quietly, and with a high degree of melancholy, "I just want them to be nice to me."

Now it was starting to make sense. Both the employee and the patient understood who was in charge, and it wasn't the patient.

Determined to Delight was initially greeted with a great deal of enthusiasm by the hospital's staff. It was maintained for about two months before participation began to wane. As with most initiatives, managers started to move back to their own comfort levels. Once they realized there was no real penalty for not participating, they cried, "I'm too busy."

The final death knell came when, looking for inspiration and a shot of momentum, Kevin asked the CEO of the hospital how his scheduled rounds were going. When he sheepishly replied that he hadn't done them, Kevin knew the program was doomed to fail. So, without fanfare or preaching, Kevin mercifully killed it. The CEO's lack of commitment to Determined to Delight would only serve to validate the growing number of managers who rationalized that they were also too busy for customers.

A nurse once said to Kevin after a customer service training session, "I don't have time for all this customer service stuff. It is my job to attend to patients." The service challenge is to get employees to relinquish the power that comes from "knowing more" and transfer it back to their customers in the form of human respect and dignity.

Counters and Glass Partitions

There are figurative barriers to customer service, such as a cold demeanor, that derive primarily from an undisciplined service culture, but there are also literal barriers that prevent a connection with the customer. Nordstrom understands this. Their employee's actions suggest that the cash register counter is a necessary evil, simply a place to conduct financial transactions. The minute the transaction is complete, they come out from behind the counter to hand shopping bags to customers, use their names, and personally thank them for their business.

The physical connection of the exchange puts it on more of a human level than most of their competitors are willing to do. It sends a power abdication message to the customer that it is not the cash register and money that's important; it is about the customer and service.

Many customers perceive the bag exchange as merely symbolic, as in, "That's a Nordstrom thing." But the gesture is more than symbolism. Nordstrom has effectively removed the counter as a barrier, thus allowing its employees to clearly establish the difference between server and customer.

On the other hand, what is the purpose of the glass partition at the doctor's office? If ever there was a physical barrier that sends a message to customers, that is it. It says to the customer or patient, "At any point in time I can close this window to block all of you out." It's amazing that these icons of days when doctors were seen as gods still exist.

Brooke was at the doctor recently and was forced to talk through the glass because the clerk was unwilling to open it. Of course this makes communication much more difficult, but it is the arrogance that stings most. The glass partition sends the exact opposite message that Nordstrom is conveying. By moving away from the counter, Nordstrom is saying, "I want you to know you are in charge." The doctor's office barrier is saying, "I want you to know I am in charge."

Tie Goes to the Customer

Anyone who has played little league baseball learned early on that "the tie goes to the runner." For those not familiar with baseball terminology, it simply means that if the ball and the runner get to first base at exactly the same time, the runner is considered safe. In customer service, the customer is the runner. If there is any question on what should be done, the employee should always defer to the customer.

Examples of this can give you a pretty good idea of the organization's culture. A shopper recently entered a Lowe's, and there was a rack of merchandise blocking part of the main aisle. A Lowe's employee was on the opposite side of the rack with a cart full of merchandise. There was only room for one to pass. He made his move first instead of signaling for the shopper to go ahead. As he went by, he looked straight ahead without the slightest effort to excuse himself. Here was an opportunity to put the customer first, and this employee failed to do so. Does this mean that all Lowe's employees would fail this test? One hopes not, but it does indicate that "customer first" is not top-of-mind to that particular employee, and it points to a lack of organizational consistency.

Tools

Identify Opportunities to Show Abdication

Identify situations where customer/employee interactions occur and encourage employees to put the customer before themselves. For example, one of our hospital clients developed standards for employee behavior on elevators to remind employees that they should relinquish space to customers out of respect. Unfortunately, what would seem like common sense, for example, letting the customer get on first, is not always exercised by employees.

Look at the Big Picture

Ask your employees to complete the following statement, "If it weren't for _____, I would be working somewhere else." If employees complete the phrase with the word patient, parents, or taxpayers, they need to be made aware that these are all customers. Ask them to consider the bigger picture to better understand that customer service is nearly everyone's business. With that comes the responsibility to treat everyone with respect and an opportunity to create a *turn on* experience.

Avoid Using Insider Terms

Employees can become so familiar with their surroundings, methods, and the people they work with that they forget that customers are not "part of the club." Employees sometimes use jargon and abbreviated terms for departments, products, or services without realizing that the customer has no idea what the employee is talking about. Teach your employees not to use insider terms with customers; encourage employees to make sure that customers understand what is being said.

Chapter 3
No Rules

> "Customers don't care how you got it done, just that you did it."
>
> —Kevin and Brooke Billingsley

Key Levels needed to support the turn on:

1. Communicate a Never-Ending Commitment to Excellence
3. Directly and Routinely Observe Employees in Action
5. Establish Accountability for Frontline Success

A long-time patient visits the doctor's office for an exam. Before she can sit down in the waiting area, she is asked to fill out a form to verify her personal information. Nothing has changed since the last time she was there, so she asks, "Can't you just indicate in your system that nothing has changed?" "No," says the clerk. "Well how come?" the patient asks. "It's a rule," she's told.

Justifying an action or inaction based on rules simply tells customers that your organization lacks flexibility, creativity, and a focus on customers. To the customer's ears, "I can't" becomes "I won't." This provides an open invitation for them to look elsewhere for the products or services they seek.

Test pilot Chuck Yeager once said, "Rules are made for people who aren't willing to make up their own." Organizations have to give employees the authority to please customers. We are not suggesting breaking all the rules for customers, but we are suggesting building flexibility into your processes and interactions so that the rules become transparent. At the very least, it needs to be an environment that says, "Unfortunately I can't do that, but here is what I can do."

If a *turn on* for customers is the flexibility of an organization to adapt to customer wants and needs, then hearing "No" is the exact opposite. Every organization needs guidelines and structures to operate, but some organizations put up barriers without understanding the consequences from the customer's perspective.

Take the classic story (or perhaps myth) of the Nordstrom's employee who took back a set of tires when Nordstrom's clearly doesn't sell tires. By most organizational standards, it would have been more realistic for the employee to say, "I'm sorry, we can't take back those tires. Our rule is that it has to be something that we actually sell." This story rang such a chord years ago because it symbolized that all things are possible in a culture that is completely dedicated to customer satisfaction. Even if you have to "eat some tires" now and then, saying "Yes" to customers will prove to be a winning strategy in the long run.

Corporate Mandates

High-performing employees who are motivated by a desire to provide excellent customer service will resent rules that in any way affect their ability to deliver that service. This inflexibility causes them to become either disenchanted or incensed. The outcome will ultimately be turnover of the organization's best customer service staff.

On the other hand, poor performers hide behind rules so that they don't have to extend themselves for customers. Sometimes even physical barriers are used to block customers, as Brooke experienced when she conducted a Thursday night meeting at the library. She had asked someone to retrieve soft drinks from the vending machines only to be told that the gate to the drinks was locked. Brooke tracked down the supervisor and explained that she was hoping to get drinks for the meeting attendees but that the gate was locked. "The gate is locked because kids were getting in there and making a mess," the supervisor said. "I can appreciate that," Brooke said, "but we are a group of adults.

If you have a key and I give you the money, do you think you could get the drinks we need?" The supervisor said, "Yeah, I guess I could do that."

As often happens, a rule was created to manage one group of difficult customers but adversely affected all customers. Instead of offering a simple solution, the supervisor forced the customer to come up with an alternative to the "no one gets in" policy.

Do your employees know they "hold the key"? Have you empowered them to use it to remove unnecessary, and perhaps unintended, barriers? Do they have a "Let me see what I can do for you" attitude?

And if you have trained and encouraged employees to use their discretion, are they "using the key" to turn a "No" into a positive solution, or do they find it safer to keep the gate closed?

Customers Are Perfectly Okay with Bending the Rules

When have you ever heard a customer complain because an employee chose to ignore a rule and cut the customer some slack? There are good and bad ways to bend the rules. Employees should be discouraged from letting customers know how lucky they are that the employee is being so generous. It takes the impetus out of the act. Customers do not see it as a "favor," they believe you are simply doing the right thing.

Kevin was excited that the new sports car he ordered arrived just in time for him to drive 3,000 miles to Florida and back. He was much less excited by the car's performance on the trip, so he took it in for servicing. The service manager informed Kevin that they were going to balance the tires, which should address the vibration problem he experienced. The service manager said that they usually charge for balancing tires after 2,500 miles, but that Kevin was in luck because they weren't going to charge him this time.

Sometimes employees say things to let the customer know they are bending the rules. That can work, but it's all in the word choice and tone of voice. In this case, Kevin didn't feel lucky or thankful. As a customer, he thought the dealership should automatically fix a problem, on a brand new car, that was never right to begin with. In this case, it would have been more impressive if the manager had simply said "There's no charge for that" without alluding to the standard policy or implying the customer was lucky.

Estes Park Pizza

A few years ago, our family was shopping while on a vacation in Colorado. The snow started coming down hard as we ducked into a pizza place on the main boulevard of Estes Park. Because it was 1:30 in the afternoon, the place was nearly empty. An unenthusiastic hostess/waitress greeted us and showed us to a table. It took less than 10 seconds to realize that this particular table was in line with the doorway, so that every time someone entered the shop from the outside, we would get blasted with a wave of cold air.

Kevin pointed to a table a bit more off to the side and asked the hostess if we could sit at the larger table away from the doorway. The waitress informed us that that was a table for eight and we did not meet the requirements. Kevin said to her, "Are you sure we can't move? It's 1:30 in the afternoon and there is no one in here." With an attitude, the waitress replied, "If you don't like it, you can tell it to the manager." Kevin told her not to bother and we walked out.

This waitress probably cost the restaurant approximately $30 because of a "rule." If we had asked for the manager, one of three things would have happened: either he would have supported the waitress, reluctantly agreed to give us the table, or cheerfully conceded to our request. However, that is almost beside the point. Somehow the hostess got it in her head that this was a "hard and fast" rule without exceptions. We are 99.9% certain that she offered to have us talk to the manager because she knows that is where the rule came from. To put this in perspective, it was more important for this pizza establishment to chill, upset, and ultimately lose income, than to give in to a simple customer request.

Think about your rules from a customer's perspective. How much latitude do your employees have to please your customers? What is the maximum amount of empowerment you will allow without invoking the "rules"? Keep in mind, every time a customer says to you, "Explain to me why you can't do that," you have reached one of those critical points where your rules are about to push a customer away.

Tools

Frontline Holds the Key

Frontline employees must be the source of your company's efforts to satisfy customers—they have the answers. They are the key. Continuously make these employees aware of their importance and involve them in the process of improving customer service.

Apologizing

Apologizing for not being able to do something is acceptable as long as employees are willing to do something in its place. However, the word "No" should be stricken from the organization's vocabulary.

Assessing Rules

Focus the organization's attention on customer feedback and direct observation to determine what rules either exist or are maintained that are unnecessarily restrictive. Unless a customer makes the organization aware that an employee abused a rule or arbitrarily erected a barrier, the organization will never know.

Chapter 4
Knowledgeable Employees

> "Knowledge has to be improved, challenged, and increased constantly, or it vanishes."
>
> —Peter Drucker

Key Levels needed to support the turn on:
1. Communicate a Never-Ending Commitment to Excellence
4. Utilize Coaching Techniques

Customers thrive on making informed decisions, so they are much more likely to be turned on by employees who are fully versed on product knowledge (what we sell), organizational knowledge (who we are), and competitive knowledge (who they are and what they sell). If your employees do not have a strong sense of where the organization is going and what their relationship is to it, then a void is created that will become the basis for negative customer perception.

In a Perfect World, Every Employee Should Be Selling

When working with clients, we emphasize that every employee in their company is a "marketing person." The executives in the room always nod their heads in agreement; they clearly understand that each employee possesses the power to retain customers and refer them to other services within the organization. However, it is one thing for an employee to provide customer service and another to be held responsible for guaranteeing future business.

Understanding this potential and doing something to foster it are also two different things. What kind of marketers are your employees? What do they really know about your products, services, and organization? Are they willing and able to deliver on that knowledge?

We are always impressed with store employees who can quickly tell customers the exact location for the most obscure products in their store. As much respect as we may have for this employee's knowledge, we have even more respect for the company and the fact that they saw fit to thoroughly train their employees on the store's products and layout.

What if your customers are so impressed with the experience at your store that they ask the person at the checkout, "How is the company's stock doing?" Technically, knowing this information has little to do with that employee's job description, but having an answer says a great deal about how involved employees are in the company's success.

A customer service provider can achieve dramatic increases in business if employees are encouraged and/or trained to take advantage of selling opportunities. In order for this to occur, three things must happen:

1. Employees must understand the benefit to the organization of making this effort.
2. They must be able to recognize a sales opportunity.
3. They must know what products and services are available within their own organization.

There is no better bang for your buck than training employees to look for opportunities to "sell" your organization. This requires a detailed analysis of what those opportunities are to ensure that customers never fall through the cracks. Organizations that are willing to put forth the extra effort to train their employees extend an invitation to customers to stay in the loop. Unlike traditional selling where the goal is to "get your business," customers see this form of selling as valuable, welcomed advice. After all, finding another provider can be hard work!

As consultants we frequently identify for our clients selling opportunities that were either exploited or missed. We've found that, on average, three times as many opportunities to sell are passed up as taken.

Businesses must look for ways to prevent this potential revenue from walking out the door. Fortunately, there are several effective solutions. We recommend giving employees daily or weekly cross-selling tips on information they can share with customers. Like restaurant servers who have tasted the special of the day, you want to provide opportunities for employees to experience what they are selling. For one client, we developed mystery shopping scenarios that would give employees a chance to direct the shopper to additional services in order to cross-sell.

Customers don't care if an employee who seemingly has all the answers, offers additional information, extends an invitation to keep in touch, and is exceedingly pleasant, is actually a "sales" person. What turns customers on is that a knowledgeable employee, with obvious pride in her work, is showing an interest in them. Quite often, however, we find that the majority of employees who consistently exhibit this type of behavior are people with sales or marketing in their titles. Why is that? The answer is they are trained to bring in revenue, and the way to do that is to represent the organization in the best possible light to customers. If they aren't able to do that, it will certainly cause them to lose their job.

For more advice on training all employees to make a sale, see Chapter 14, "Helping Customers Make Decisions."

Top 100 Hospital

A client of ours, designated as a Top 100 Hospital in Orthopedics, hung large banners all around the campus, proudly proclaiming its award. Our firm decided to take advantage of these visible signs of organizational pride and test employees on their knowledge of the Top 100 designation. Our reasoning was that if this visible effort is intended to reach consumers, then employees should be prepared to provide more detailed information to curious customers.

Six employees were randomly mystery shopped and asked about their knowledge of the Top 100 designation. Four of the employees did not know why their hospital had received the award or what the award represented; one said it was for Orthopedics but could not give any details other than to say the criteria was stringent; and the sixth employee thought it was for patient care. Was there an effort to inform employees of either the award or the corresponding marketing effort? Did it get lost amidst the hundreds of other messages that day? Are the employees numb or oblivious to self-promotion? Whatever the reason that allowed employees to remain uninformed of this accomplishment, the unfortunate result is that their ignorance or ambivalence is passed on to the consumer, only to the customer it looks like a lack of competence and not caring about the job.

Organizations must educate employees on what they intend to share with the community. The goal must always be to turn employees into ambassadors for the company. It is not enough for your marketing people to get the message out; they must be certain that the message is being received and understood. After a new message is released internally to your organization, or a new campaign is launched, we recommend making random calls to employees to ask them what they know about it. Did they get the message, what did they think it said, and how do they intend to use the information?

As an example, let's say your company is acquiring a competitor and you need to inform your employees before the information is released to the press and your customers. Instead of just simply informing your employees of the purchase, it would be advantageous for you to prepare some specific talking points on the benefits of the merger so that employees can answer the inevitable questions from customers who want to know how to the merger will affect them.

"Because Word of Mouth Is Just Too Slow"

There is an ad agency in Indianapolis whose slogan is "Because word of mouth is just too slow." Is it really? Would one ever need to do traditional marketing if one combined a well-orchestrated internal promotional blitz with world-class customer service? Let everyone who comes in contact with your organization know what you are up to, let them come in and experience the best you have to offer, and let them tell everyone else.

An example of this occurred when a hospital system announced that it was planning to build a new satellite hospital in a growing part of the market. As is often the case, the competition was doing the same thing less than a mile away and had an eight-month lead.

Before the first brick is laid, the organization should make certain that every customer contact employee working at the other locations in the market knows, at least in general terms, all the services that will be offered at the new facility, when it will be open, and the reason for building there.

Employees should also realize that with this information come expectations. They will be required to share their knowledge with everyone they come in contact with, especially if the people they are talking to live in the vicinity of the new facility. "Mrs. Smith, are you aware we are building a new facility on your side of town? Now, if you like, you can have your blood tested there once it opens. I can call you when we have more information on the schedule, would that be okay?"

Because employees may be questioning why they need to go to all the effort to communicate this information to customers, there should also be opportunities for employees to talk to managers and co-workers to share common knowledge and strategies. They may ask themselves, "Why do I care if we have a new facility?"

Here is an opportunity to test the "word of mouth is too slow" theory. The hospital could announce that it was going to reduce advertising dollars because it was going to rely on employees to spread the word. A portion of the dollars that would have been spent on advertising could go into a referral program. The savings would go into a pool to be shared with employees when bonafide referral candidates turn into customers. Employees who traditionally cry that marketing is just wasted money would love nothing more than to see advertising dollars go in their pockets.

Tools

Use Information Confidently

Encourage employees to exhibit confidence in the information they give to customers. This can come only from the knowledge of knowing who does what, what is occurring at the organization, the company's mission, and its entire line of products and services.

Look for Selling/Cross-Selling Opportunities

It is not realistic to expect selling or cross-selling to occur with every encounter. Employees need to be prepared to pick the right message and the right moment. Here are some tips:

- Train staff to become more active listeners so that they can better identify customer needs.
- Conduct role-playing exercises on how to identify selling opportunities.
- Teach staff to be more assertive with potential customers.
- Communicate the financial benefit to the organization of cross-selling existing services.
- Reward employees for selling/cross-selling services by allowing them to share in any additional revenues that are generated.

Provide Thorough Answers

Customers know when an employee stops short of providing them with a solution to a problem. They also know when an employee has an opportunity to find someone who does have an answer and doesn't take it. Customers assume employees have answers. For instance, when we ask an employee at the office supply store where the packing tape is, we expect him to know it is Aisle 9 on the lower right-hand side. When customers receive vague answers to questions, they often presume employee disinterest, or worse, they believe they are intentionally being prevented from getting information.

Chapter 5

Employees Who Like to Serve

> "You'll know you are fully committed to service excellence when you are willing to hire someone because of it, and fire someone over it."
>
> —Kevin and Brooke Billingsley

Key Levels needed to support the turn on:

1. Communicate a Never-Ending Commitment to Excellence
2. Hire People Who Want to Serve Others

A mystery shopper of ours made a telephone call and concluded that the employee she spoke with "sounded like she liked her job." This phrase has always stuck with us because without even hearing the call, we can imagine what it sounded like. Customers are turned on when employees have a genuine sparkle in their eye for the customer or a tone in their voice that indicates it is more than a job to them.

Your Customers Are on to You

Customers know the customer service culture of your organization better than you do. Through multiple encounters over time, they get to experience all of your superstars, your slackers, and everyone in between. They analyze multiple encounters and keep a running mental scorecard. When the score drops below an acceptable level, they disappear. To make matters worse, 96 percent of your departing customers leave without a trace; no letter of explanation, no new terms and conditions, and no forwarding address.

Organizations that truly believe in customer service must be prepared to dismiss every employee who did not at least smile at each and every customer. If customers want and expect respect or at least a sign that their presence has value, that is where every service provider should begin. Employees unwilling to live by the simple standards of acknowledgment and pleasantness will have to work elsewhere.

Is this too harsh a sentence for non-smilers? If your organization were to take customer acknowledgment from a suggestion to a job-threatening mandate, we guarantee an immediate rise in customer satisfaction. The service standards you set in place should be your organization's Ten Commandments. They are the basis from which you grow to another level; they should not be something you struggle to maintain.

Those who see the glass as half empty will say, "We train them, but it doesn't last," or "Service workers are hard to come by, especially good ones," or "It is difficult to know when employees aren't performing to expectations." Customer service training is not like the training an accountant receives on the latest tax laws. Once tax law knowledge is put into action, it usually becomes second nature to the practitioner. Customer service training is different in that, even though one can be trained on how knowledge should be delivered, going from knowledge to action must first go through a complex web of human relations. Think of tax law as inanimate and customer service as animate. Customer service is a moving target.

Saboteurs, Inanimate Objects, and Attention Seekers

Another way to classify employment candidates is to put them in one of three categories: Saboteurs, Inanimate Objects, and Attention Seekers.

Some people spread malcontent while insisting that no one provides better service than they do. We call these employees *Saboteurs*. They are the individuals who, with animated nods of approval, "support" the service program while secretly holding to their own selfish agendas. Saboteurs are aggressive and may appear eager to please, but watch out;

their enthusiasm hides their true contempt for customers. They are willing to show their disdain for customers if they see fit and have no problem putting customers "in their place." Saboteurs lie in wait for the opportunity to say "I told you so" when initiatives run out of steam.

To weed the Saboteurs out of your list of candidates, look at each applicant's track record. You will likely find a lot of past jobs as others grew tired of their destructive natures. Ask about their service philosophy. Look for the focus to be on them and how good they believe they are, not about their dedication to the customer. Allow them to relay a story about a customer that upset them. The examples given will speak volumes about their tolerance level with customers.

Inanimate Objects are the people who don't want to be noticed. If they are not animated during the hiring process, they surely will not be with customers, either. Look for a sign that their energy will be sustainable. Keep the interview focused on their approaches to customers using what-if situations. The key will be to see if candidates get frustrated when the challenge becomes uncomfortable. You need to adopt an "if you can't stand the heat, get out of the kitchen" approach. Employees who genuinely care about serving customers will accept the challenge and reveal their creativity.

If you do not perceive anything special about that person, you can bet customers will feel that way, too. How will he or she ever exceed customer expectations if they don't exceed yours?

Attention Seekers, however, force customers to stand up and take notice. They are "on" all of the time because they get a thrill out of the response from customers. In order to be consistently up, these candidates have found ways to achieve results regardless of feelings or uncomfortable circumstances.

Make sure that an Attention Seeker's goals are in keeping with the organization's mission. Ask applicants what it is about customer relationships that give them the greatest pleasure, and what would be an example of exceeding a customer's expectations.

Avoid hiring someone because he or she is "bubbly." It is not enough to be high-spirited. True Attention Seekers will want to explain why they do what they do. They will likely share a philosophy born out of experience, an interest in human behavior, and a passion for applying that knowledge.

Hire People Who Want to Be Noticed

In order to change the customer service culture, managers must first begin to hire people who possess a visible spark during the interview. The spark will be seen in the candidate's eyes, the confidence in the way she carries herself, and the strength of voice. If you can find people who will at least look you in the eye, you have half the battle won.

Additional things to look for when hiring for customer service are:

- Did the candidate smile during the interview?
- Can the candidate verbalize a personal philosophy on service, and does it fit with the organization's philosophy?
- Does the candidate possess enough energy to get through the day and through irritable customers?
- Can he or she act? Is the candidate comfortable becoming someone else when he or she doesn't feel like serving?
- Is the candidate entrepreneurial-minded? If allowed to do so, can he or she handle things alone?

Remember that people who provide mediocre service get no satisfaction from being noticed. They meld into the woodwork, refusing to be special. Customers don't comment about them positively or negatively, because there is never anything extraordinary to talk about. These employees are not awful, they just never put themselves in a position to stand out. They do not want attention, for reasons only they can explain. They hide their personalities, reserving them only for people they genuinely care about. Unfortunately, those people are never the customers.

One may think that these employees present no risks. The tendency may be to leave them alone because they are not doing any real damage, but only extraordinary service allows the organization to press forward.

Message to New Hires

It is important for employees to be educated on your customer service expectations from the first minute they walk in the door. For instance, several of our clients require employment candidates to view a video on their customer service philosophy.

The beginning of a new job is the beginning of a relationship between the company and the employer. Those first few days and weeks are critical to your employee's long-term satisfaction in the job. By educating them properly from day one, you help assure they will succeed, which is a win for them, a win for you, and a win for your customers.

Ask yourself how much time is devoted to sharing your organization's customer service philosophy with new hires. We don't mean reciting the mission statement from the employee manual or the annual report; we are referring to a daily reminder from management on the organization's values in the form of suggestions, coaching, observations, or praise.

Did you hear the following when you were interviewed for your job?

"It is important that you know up front that we are completely dedicated to serving the customer. There is absolutely nothing more important. We appreciate and respect customers for what they mean to all of us, and we do not accept any behavior that is not completely pro-customer. We also believe in going out of our way for customers every chance we get, because we want to see them again and again. Each time they come in contact with us, we take appropriate steps to strengthen their relationship with us. We want them to perceive us as contributing to a better life for them and their families."

Sound familiar? We didn't think so. But what organization would disagree with this pro-customer sentiment? An unending commitment to customer service begins with an unending commitment to educate and train employees, and that commitment is especially important in the beginning of an employee's relationship with you.

"If they make me do one more thing for customers, I'll quit!"

An employee once declared in one of our customer service training sessions, "If they make me do one more thing for customers, I'll quit!"

Needless to say, our client's management team found this statement disturbing. But what was she really saying? We believe she was sending the message that customers are major disruptions that keep her from doing her "real" job.

Nowhere in her statement is she saying that the customer is important or that she is already doing the best she can. Apparently, no one had ever made it clear that *customers are her job*! If this employee had understood her role, going to customer service training would only have enhanced her current efforts, not added increased frustration.

Employees Are More Aware of Their Shortcomings Than Managers Think

Our consultancy did a customer service training session for a client, and things were not progressing the way Kevin had hoped. The group was not opening up, so he asked them, "If you knew you were going to be disciplined tomorrow for something service-related you did today, what might that be?"

This woke up the crowd. Without any managers present (which is an important fact), Kevin went around the room and got responses from each attendee such as "I know I could smile more," "I could give better eye contact," and "I could get along better with co-workers." It was clear that they all knew what their shortcomings were. This begs the question, why were they not giving 100 percent, and why were they free to maintain this behavior?

It is important for managers to address employee behavior through observation. The goal is to expose behavior that has been tolerated in the past and meet it with a new strategy that states, "You know what you are doing; now, I know. Together we need to make some changes."

Perception Strategies has had tremendous success with a program that uses observation in the form of mystery shopping to evaluate employees individually. This program allows managers to use aggregate data and shopper narratives for each employee on the manager's staff based on a minimum number of mystery shops over a given period of time. This information allows the manager to specifically coach employees on their strengths and weaknesses rather than looking at departmental scores. It also eliminates the excuses used by employees to deflect criticism because no proof was available.

"Being a waiter in Europe is like being an attorney in the States."

When we took a Caribbean cruise on a Celebrity ship last year, the service culture on that ship was so much better than what we were accustomed to that we sought out Leann Davis, who it was announced held the newly created position of Director of Training and Development on board.

When we met with her, we said that we noticed that the staff consisted of very few Americans to which Leann, a Canadian, clarified that only three out of the thousand or so employees on board the ship were Americans. She explained that most of the staff was European and that in Europe customer service is seen differently. She said, "Being a waiter there is like being an attorney in the States." She further explained that Europeans take a great deal of pride in serving others and that other Europeans hold servers in very high regard.

Contrast that with the state of customer service in the United States where management often cannot or will not take the time to teach remedial service skills. This creates an enormous gap between what organizations say they want and what management is producing on the frontline.

We only have ourselves to blame. America has created the next generation of bad service providers. Some of us teach our kids how to recognize great service—and complain when they don't get it—but we're afraid that today's youth aren't being supplied with the skills needed to turn that recognition into a competitive advantage or a true desire to serve others. They have not heard the speech:

> You are now ready my son to meet the needs and wants of other human beings. If you do so with selfless respect for others, you will not only be recognized and rewarded for your efforts, you will also gain the satisfaction of knowing that you can be great at whatever you choose to do.

If we don't train the next generation of customer service workers now, then we won't be happy when we're later forced to reap what we have sown.

Waves of Attitude

What employees share with loved ones about their work is often what they are communicating to customers. Scary thought, isn't it? The accumulation of opinions regarding the boss, co-workers, job responsibilities, corporate mandates, and the customers themselves comes across in subtle, and not so subtle, "waves of attitude." It is virtually impossible for an employee to detest his job but show the utmost respect for the customer.

These waves of attitude do not have to be negative. Some organizations have painstakingly developed a culture that consistently displays a genuine interest in serving customers. Organizations are finally coming around to the realization that customer service is a differentiating factor worth exploiting. It all starts with hiring the right people and then properly training them. However, despite the development of comprehensive programs to make the work environment more customer-focused, some companies avoid the tough decisions related to employees who are not on board with the program. As a result, when these well-intentioned initiatives are launched, employees who simply give it lip service are allowed to continue working, slowly poisoning the company's customers and other employees.

On the other hand, being the employee who provides exceptional customer service can be a lonely undertaking. There are only two ways in which the person who passionately enjoys serving others can survive: 1) They find a culture that supports their needs; and/or 2) They possess the strength of character to shine, in the face of all adversity, and by doing so make others look bad.

Will the latter raise the bar for other employees? That depends on what management does. Unfortunately, it is unreasonable to assume that the manager who created the poor work environment will recognize that it is a poor work environment. And in most cases, it is not worth the hassle for the service-minded employee to endure the loneliness. He or she usually moves on in search of a more customer-friendly culture.

What if a manager could actually use this employee's passion as leverage? To do this, managers should interview the employee to learn the secret and determine why they do what they do. Then, elevate their status by inviting them to coach others.

Tools

Discover "Champions"

While much less involved than a "Going the Extra Mile" award program, the following is a brief coaching exercise for managers, designed to identify staff who exhibit certain customer service characteristics. This exercise can be done in a group setting or one-on-one. The intent is to hold up for emulation those who best exhibit the kind of behavior desired, and to immediately begin discussing change with those who do not.

Ask the participants to take a few minutes to jot down the people in their daily circle who best exemplify (or champion) the following behaviors and skills:

- Acknowledgment
- Apologizing
- Empathy

- Smiling
- Eye Contact
- Follow Through
- Kindness
- Tone of Voice
- Selling the Organization

Ask them to share examples of how these characteristics are demonstrated. Without mentioning names, ask them to give some thought to those who least exemplify these behaviors or skills. Discuss what it would take for everyone to achieve the customer service being provided by the champions.

Chapter 6
Engaging the Customer

> "Let us be grateful to people who make us happy, they are the charming gardeners who make our souls blossom."
>
> —Marcel Proust

Key Levels needed to support the turn on:
  2. Hire People Who Want to Serve Others
  3. Directly and Routinely Observe Employees in Action
  4. Utilize Coaching Techniques
  5. Establish Accountability for Frontline Success

It's near midnight and we have just gotten off a plane in Raleigh, North Carolina. Exhausted, we pull into a Clarion Hotel and stand at the empty counter for several minutes. Finally, a voice from the back of the office yells, "You'll have to wait a minute, I'm working on something." After that minute turned into five, we were rewarded for our patience with complete silence—no directions, no information on the free breakfast, and definitely no "thank you" for choosing Clarion Hotels.

Being engaging means that employees are focused and in the moment. We like to call this skill "managing the moment." Effective employees purposefully look for ways to relate to customers by raising their antennae and being "on" throughout the encounter. This creates a warm bond with the customer and an opportunity for a relationship to develop on some level. Customers are willing to open up to employees who do not erect barriers that say, "I am on this side of the counter and you are on that side. Let's keep it that way."

Starbucks has as its Core Purpose "to provide an uplifting experience that enriches peoples' lives." To support that mission, they instill 5 Behaviors in their employees, one of which is "be genuine." Being genuine means to "connect, discover, and respond" to the customer—in other words, engage.

We recently put this to the test at Paramount's Kings Island, an amusement park outside of Cincinnati. At nine o'clock at night we were looking at a two-hour drive home, so we decided to load up on some caffeine at the Starbucks located inside the park. With a line flowing out the door, Kevin finally reached the counter only to be met by some of the most chipper and engaging employees he has ever encountered, especially for nine o'clock. Nothing was rote—it was simply free-flowing great service.

True to their Core Purpose, it was clear that Starbucks had reached the apex of customer service: training employees to be themselves while being engaging on an individual customer level. What was most fascinating was witnessing this behavior from young people who were plucked from the same pool of candidates the rest of the park utilized, but with strikingly different results.

It is unrealistic for employees to be engaging to everyone; after all, not everyone appreciates it. People want different things out of customer service—some want employees to be outgoing and others don't. That is why it is possible for employees to receive two completely different responses from the exact same scenario. For instance, some customers want employees to ask if there is anything they can help them with. Without that effort, customers find it frustrating to have to seek out employees when they do have questions.

Other customers truly resent being constantly asked by employees if there is anything they can help them with. These are the people who say "Just looking" before retail employees finish asking the question. Some of us can flip back and forth between appreciating it and resenting it. However, employees must always err on the side of "over-helping"; commission is preferable to omission every time.

The best customer service providers know how to engage customers by:

1. Locking in early.

2. Reading the situation and the customer.
3. Engaging or letting go depending on how the customer responds.

The concept of locking in early suggests that employees are focused on the customer from the very start. Employees must immediately give eye contact, smile at the customer, and say something conversational like "Hi, how's your day going?" How customers respond to this type of question will tell the employee if there is an opportunity for a *turn on* experience. If customers answer the question either in a positive way with "Great, I can't believe I finally found this book" or negatively with "Lousy, I've been all over town and can't find a decent skirt," an opening has been created for employees to engage.

The *turn on* for customers comes when employees respond with something helpful such as, "We have a newsletter I would be happy to sign you up for so you get notified of all new book releases" or "I'm sorry you've had a lousy day. If you tell me what you're looking for, perhaps I can make some recommendations."

A phrase that is commonly used in these situations is "Did you find everything okay?" This one baffles us. What are they going to do if we say "No"? We are tempted to respond with, "Nope, I'm here at the register with merchandise on the counter and money in my hand because there were five other things I couldn't find." Customers resent being asked goofy, nonsensical questions that have no chance of enhancing the employee/customer relationship because they weren't meant to be answered in the first place.

Sometimes employees misread customers and plow ahead when they should let go and find an alternate way to make the experience memorable. A classic example is a waiter who, despite observing animated discussions at his customers' table, decides that he will interrupt anyway to see if the customers want something like more bread. In that case, the best way to create turned on customers is to find a way, such as impeccable timing, to make the experience memorable that doesn't include interrupting the flow of conversation.

Abercrombie and Fitch

Our youngest son Jordan got caught up in the whole Abercrombie and Fitch experience when he was in high school. So when Christmas rolled around, at the top of his list was more A&F.

Trying hard not to show our respective ages, but nonetheless struck by some of the large, unclothed images on the wall and the blaring music coming from the sound system, we entered the store with his wish list in hand.

As marketing people, we get it, we really do. And our son helps to remind us that this experience is not intended to be for us. But here is where it goes wrong for us. Perhaps it was just freaky timing, but everyone in the store at that time was our age, doing the same thing we were, buying for our kids. After all, we're the ones with the money. Where would this new generation of mega-consumers be without us?

We don't expect A&F to cater to us, but here is what we do want. We want a policy of customer service where the young 20-somethings who are working in the store are allowed to and/or are capable of waiting on us, not just refold shirts and pants. Our experience was the complete opposite of being engaging. And it wasn't just that we were ignored; when we did ask for assistance they were helpless to help us.

The conversation went something like this:

"We really like the shirt on the mannequin, but there doesn't seem to be any on the racks. Can you get that one down for us?"

"I can't do that."

"How come?"

"It's a rule. You might be able to get it at another Abercrombie and Fitch store."

15 seconds pass.

"Can you make a call to see if they have it?"

"I guess so."

Where would A&F be if the funds from parents dried up? The notion that bad service is somehow cool may fly with kids, but it is still unacceptable with our generation, and it is setting an awful precedent for future generations.

Even companies like A&F that understand what the youth market needs should train their employees to be generationally flexible. Apply the hands-off approach with kids and turn on the charm with parents.

Scripts Are Not Engaging

Many organizations supply their employees with scripts on how to initially interact with customers such as, "Good morning, XYZ Company, this is John Smith." The concept of scripting is designed to help employees remember to use the basic customer service standards and to create consistency.

Unfortunately, organizations that stop at scripting and go no further fail to understand that customer perception is less about what is delivered, and more about how it is presented. Being engaging trumps scripting every time in the eyes of customers. Think about it. If you are on the other end of the phone line and an employee addresses you in a disinterested monotone, are you impressed that they got the script right?

Let's take it a step further. Imagine you're the department manager who had a customer go out of her way to seek you out and tell you emphatically that, "A little while ago I spoke on the telephone with an employee in your department who clearly has a bad attitude." Surprised, you say, "Really, what did he say?" "Well it was just awful," the flustered customer says, "He said in this awful tone, 'Good morning, XYZ Company, this is John Smith.'" This customer's complaint is further proof that it is more in how it is said and less in what is said.

Lowe's Again

An example of managers not knowing whether their employees are making any effort to engage customers occurred on a trip that two shoppers took to Lowe's. It seems the employees at the registers showed signs that they were able to speak, because they did to one another.

Unfortunately, they could not utter one syllable to the two shoppers. One shopper was so fed up with the service that she called to speak to the manager when she got back home. When the manager got on the line, the shopper expressed her concern about how she had felt neglected, which she perceived as the employee's blatant contempt for the customer. He listened and apologized for the occurrence. He then said, "If people like you would just call and tell us, we would know it was going on."

Whatever happened to the power of observation? As busy as managers are, a large portion of their time must be spent observing their employees to ensure that the customer service standards that were trained are still in place. Did someone, at some time, instruct these employees to engage the customer? Of course they did. The question is, however, when did these employees decide to ignore it? And who was there to tell them it was unacceptable?

In addition to manager observations, one of the most effective methods Perception Strategies has at its disposal for observing employees is mystery shopping. We like to tell people that mystery shopping is a rehearsal that allows clients to see things before they happen to real customers.

We sometimes hear from organizations who say that they are thinking about doing their own mystery shopping program using employees, including managers. That is a lot of pressure to put on employees, and no matter how hard they try, their own people are not objective. They simply cannot see it from the customer's perspective. Brooke likes to use this analogy: Let's say you have lived in your home for at least five years—are visitors going to perceive it the same way you do? Chances are their senses will pick up the smells, the sounds, and the clutter you have unknowingly accepted. The same is true for allowing employees to assess your service culture. Their senses have understandably dulled over time.

Mystery shoppers are customers with heightened senses. They don't accept things because that's the way it has always been. They take an organization's service standards at face value. If the organization goes to the trouble of creating values and communicating those values to the entire workforce, they should have customers freshly evaluate adherence. Using the feedback of those you hope to influence is the only true way to effectively evaluate customer service excellence.

Tools

Engage Customers on Their Own Terms

- When customers walk in the door, employees should approach them as soon as possible.
- Instruct employees on the need to appreciate customer differences and to identify the type of customer they are working with.

Show Enthusiasm

Know that it is not just what you say, but how you say it, that drives customer perception. Consumers are rarely prepared to hear "Of course I can!" so say it as often as possible.

Make Eye Contact

Eye contact is essential to showing respect for the customer and establishing a relationship. When eye contact is lacking, it conveys disinterest and an uncaring attitude.

Smile

A genuine smile has a way of touching a customer's heart. It is a reflection of how the employee feels about himself/herself and about the job they are doing.

Hold Your Employees Accountable

- Interview employees who have been observed as unfriendly to understand their source of unhappiness and present them with alternatives.
- Observe employees in action with customers.
- Evaluate whether or not the right employees are dealing with customers.
- Videotape customers on what is important to them and use it in training.
- Conduct a class of "Acting 101: Fake it 'til you make it" so that employees can practice until it becomes natural.

Chapter 7
Employee Creativity

> "Creativity involves breaking out of established patterns in order to look at things in a different way."
>
> —Edward de Bono

Key Levels needed to support the turn on:

2. Hire People Who Want to Serve Others
6. Reward Those Who Excel in Customer Service

Few of the *turn ons* in this book are tied to an organization's culture more than an employee's creativity on behalf of customers. Customers are *turned on* by employees who care enough to come up with creative solutions and add a personal element to their customer service that is uniquely theirs. However, this is only possible if employees are allowed to be expressive and find solutions on their own.

The Spa Lesson

A man walked in from the pouring rain and into a day spa with a small child in tow. He explained to the receptionist that his wife was coming in for a massage the following day. He pulled a credit card out of his wallet and said he wanted to surprise her by paying for it ahead of time. Staring blankly, the receptionist said, "I can't ring up a sale today for tomorrow." She said that she could write something down as a reminder but that it would be better if he came back again tomorrow. The husband looked defeated as he turned and walked out the door.

Listening to the interaction, Brooke approached the receptionist and took exception with her less-than-stellar customer service efforts. "This man went out of his way to do something special for his wife," Brooke said, "and the best you could do is tell him to come back later?" She asked the receptionist why she couldn't take the credit card information and then have someone ring it up in the morning. "I guess I could have done that," the receptionist said sheepishly. She was obviously not approaching this situation with a creative problem-solving attitude.

It is probably safe to say that the receptionist never uses creativity to find solutions. Therefore, it is also safe to assume that the spa has not created a culture of creativity. If the receptionist had the desire or if the proper environment had been in place, she could have easily turned the customer on with very little effort. All she had to say was, "I can't ring up a sale today for tomorrow, but because this is such a special occasion, I am going to take care of this personally for you. All I need is a little information and you will be all set. I'm also going to throw in a special gift for your wife."

How could the customer perceive this as anything but an extraordinary effort? The receptionist appears to be a caring person who wants to do something special for the customer. And yet, aside from the gift, which the spa could easily incorporate into every gift certificate situation, Brooke's simple suggestion of writing down the financial information is all the receptionist would have to do.

As the Edward de Bono quote at the beginning of this chapter suggests, the receptionist needed to look at the encounter in a different, pro-customer way and use proactive language to elicit a positive, "tell others about it" impression.

Susan's Dive

Back in 1998, Susan was one of our consultancy's original mystery shoppers. Once upon a time she had worked with Kevin in the healthcare field. In fact, it was her idea to recruit community actors as mystery shoppers because, as a talented actress herself, she had access to a pool of actors. We have been following her suggestion ever since.

One of Susan's assignments called for her to make an appointment at an outpatient diagnostic center. Because it was an icy winter day and the sidewalk was not properly cleared, Susan decided to spice up the shop by rolling in the snow to suggest a slip on the ice. Holding her newly injured wrist, with tears to match, she proceeded inside making every employee within earshot aware of her fall.

After explaining at great length how and why she fell, the staff's response was to take Susan to a physician's office in the building, where they refused to see her because she was not a patient. They then provided her with a telephone number deferring her to the person who owned the building. As a final act, she was referred to the competition's urgent care center located in a building nearby.

Were these actions justified because they were following the rules? A case could be made that because of liability concerns they did nothing wrong. But from a customer service perspective they also didn't do anything right, nor did they show creativity. Their actions suggest that they wanted her "problem" to disappear instead of "keeping her in the loop" and showing her that they valued the relationship. The creative thing to do would have been to take it upon themselves to get Susan the care she needed while at the same time keeping her as a customer.

But that is not the end of the story. Susan got in her car and drove to the main hospital to share with them what had happened at the outpatient clinic. When she relayed her experience to someone at the front desk, she was quickly introduced to a hospital administrator who personally handled Susan's case to its conclusion. If liability was a concern, the hospital dealt with it proactively instead running away from it.

Unique Service Shticks

What is a unique service "shtick?" It is the collection of phrases that an employee uses on a consistent basis to connect with the customer and turn them on. A classic example would be calling everyone "honey" or "sweetie." If used inappropriately, unique service shticks are risky because they increase the probability that people will dislike the employee, and hence the business. It is very easy to cross a generational or gender line and unintentionally offend the customer.

A unique service shtick is often an employee's sincere interpretation of great customer service. However, when overused, it is best that a manager take the employee aside, thank them for this extraordinary effort to relate to customers, and coach them on when it is or is not appropriate. It is easy for a manager to say, "Oh, that's just Dorothy's thing," out of fear that they will deflate the employee's perceived enthusiasm. Managers often find the risk of bursting an employee's bubble greater than offending a customer. They choose to follow the route of least immediate pain. They have to work with their employees every day, but they don't necessarily have to deal with customers directly.

Kevin personally likes service shticks—he'll take a "honey" any day—but it becomes less effective and downright annoying when the employee works for an organization you frequent on a regular basis. The jig is up when customers realize that this employee uses the same approach for everyone. It stops being cute really fast. Subliminally, customers know that the unique service shtick is often being used as a substitution for genuinely personal service.

In a customer service training class we conducted, we posed the question, "What is one thing you could change to make the service you provide better?" One of the participants said, "Well, I sing in front of customers all the time. I'm a singer. That's just what I do." This response was out of left field because she was not really telling us what she was willing to change, but rather what she was unwilling to change. This was kind of a unique service shtick in reverse, because she was not singing for the customer's benefit. She was going to do it whether anyone liked it or not. It seemed to be more a coping mechanism than a substitution for genuine personal service.

Unique service shticks must be creative, non-redundant, and appropriate in order to be effective. If you frequent a Sam's Club store, you know that when you exit the store, an employee compares the items you have purchased to your receipt. One of the "exiters" at our Sam's Club utilizes a unique service shtick when he focuses on one item or creates a theme based on whatever you buy such as, "Have a great picnic," or, "Don't stay up too late with that adding machine," or "Your cats are obviously very big eaters." We originally thought this was something this particular Sam's Club store trained their employees to do. Then, after about the tenth trip, we realized this was *his* thing. We realize this could be annoying to some, but we find ourselves looking forward to what he is going to say next.

Tools

Use a Sense of Humor

Encourage employees to use their sense of humor with customers. While it is not something one can train, humor helps to connect with customers on a personal level. If you know an employee has a playful side, encourage them to let it out for customers. When used appropriately, it is almost always a sure way to create a positive experience.

Encourage Creativity with Stipulations

- Give employees some latitude to do "their own thing," but only after they have mastered your organization's basic standards. They must first prove that they can consistently present a positive perception before they take some risks.
- Once it is observed, managers should discuss with more creative employees their intent with the style they use. Keep it light, though. This discussion should be an opportunity to tweak the creativity if it is a little over the top or to determine if it is something this employee would be willing to share in order to encourage other employees.

Chapter 8
Teamwork

"Teamwork is no accident. It is the by-product of good leadership."

—John Adair

"The best teamwork comes from men who are working independently toward one goal in unison."

—James Cash Penney

Key Levels needed to support the turn on:

1. Communicate a Never-Ending Commitment to Excellence
2. Hire People Who Want to Serve Others
3. Directly and Routinely Observe Employees in Action

It is a *turn on* when employees work together to get things done for customers. To be successful, employees must share the common goal of pleasing the customer. The primary challenge is achieving a delicate balance among employees because nearly everyone is sensitive to being taken advantage of. Employees must have confidence in their fellow workers as in "I've got your back," rather than feeling that the people they work with will not reciprocate by helping out when they need it.

Take customer hand-offs for example. **Rule #1** of customer service teamwork is to allow customer hand-offs only if the other employee is more qualified; otherwise, handle the customer yourself. It will not be appreciated by either the customer or the other employee if the hand-off occurs only out of convenience for the employee, as in, "It's time for me to punch out."

Customers would prefer to deal with one person, but if they perceive that they are going to get better service with a team approach they will accept it. Therefore, **Rule #2** is to work as a team, especially if it is going to add value to the customer. For instance, avoid having employees say, "I'm not really sure, let me give Jerry a call, he might have an idea." To the customer, this is simply wasted time with no end in sight.

It is critical for managers to maintain balance among employees, which brings us to **Rule #3**—create open dialogue among team members regarding customer care. Establish some ground rules to make sure employees are clear on what they can and cannot do with other employees or for other employees. Give them a forum for addressing concerns so that they never speak negatively of other employees or blame one another in front of customers.

Showroom Teamwork

A salesman approached Brooke on the showroom floor of a large furniture store and asked if he could help her. Initially she said she was just looking, but when the salesman approached a second time she asked if the chair she was looking at came in any other fabrics. He said, "No, the chair came directly from China, which is why it is so reasonably priced."

A female salesperson overheard the conversation and explained to Brooke that there was a similar chair by an American manufacturer that cost a little more but had a variety of fabrics. She excused herself and retrieved the book of fabrics for Brooke to review.

Brooke took note of how this salesperson's intervention affected the first salesperson, especially given that most furniture showroom employees are on commission. He not only didn't get mad that another employee was chiming in, they quickly approached this potential sale like a team.

From the customer's perspective, the female employee showed that she cared more about serving the customer by providing additional information than she cared about potentially upsetting her colleague. Another positive aspect of this encounter was that the store had successfully created an animosity-free environment that allowed the salespeople to work together to achieve the best customer service outcome.

Guest Partners

A healthcare client of ours adopted a unique approach to patient care by assigning a certain number of hospital rooms to employees they called "Guest Partners." These Guest Partners are responsible for all of the patient's needs (except clinical care) such as serving meals, responding to specific patient requests, and cleaning rooms.

When this program was first described to us, we immediately thought how grateful the patients must be for the additional attention. We were right—patients did respond favorably to the program. We had to ask ourselves, why then, was the hospital asking us to conduct customer service training for the Guest Partners when it seemed they were so effective?

We soon learned that the employees hired to implement this unique program were suffering from an inferiority complex. They performed a valued service that was appreciated by customers, but they didn't see it that way. In conversations with Guest Partner managers, we discovered that, either directly or indirectly, nurses were keeping Guest Partner staff "in their place" by failing to recognize them as teammates. Even though the duties performed by staff allowed nurses to do more of what they were trained to do, the Guest Partners were made to feel like second-class citizens when compared to the clinical side of patient care. Sadly, the Guest Partners did not consider positive customer feedback as the benchmark for measuring success. Instead, they were looking for respect from the nurses, but they weren't getting any.

It is imperative for managers to constantly focus on the most important target: the customers. As hard as it may be, especially in light of daily working conditions, managers must convince employees that peer recognition is secondary to customer satisfaction. One of the best ways to do this is to regularly share all verbal and written customer comments with staff. It is also beneficial to provide management in the other areas with the same information to give them a stronger sense of the area or department's value to customers. A culture of teamwork must also be fostered among all employees, regardless of each employee's perceived rank or duties.

Paradox: Most Employees Think They're Great!

Years ago, Kevin was responsible for conducting an employee satisfaction survey, which this client conducted every two or three years. From this undertaking he learned that employees, on the whole, believe that:

1. "I do a wonderful job and have graded myself accordingly."
2. "If I am required to work with you at times, but you are not in my department, you're just 'okay.'"
3. "If you work in a department other than mine and I have no reason to interact with you, I question why the organization bothers to pay for all that 'dead weight.'"

That is not a very sophisticated analysis, but nonetheless pretty accurate. We meet a lot of employees in our customer service training who think they are very good at what they do. Then we either observe them ourselves or mystery shop them and find out they are not half as good as they think they are. Those who are the most vocal are often the ones who use their aggressiveness as a defense mechanism, and those who are the most negative on the telephone don't identify themselves to the customer.

Conversely, other departments are not half as bad as employees think. However, this internal mindset of "us versus them" is a serious deterrent to great customer service. Animosity between departments is felt by customers through finger-pointing and excuses—none of which interests the customer.

Respect for other areas of the organization must be visible to customers in order for teamwork to become a customer turn on. Customers enjoy seeing employees work like a fine-tuned track relay team, especially if that is what it takes to get them what they need. That is much preferred to seeing employees roll their eyes at being inconvenienced by the request of another employee.

The latter is more likely to occur if the employees do not know or respect one another. Periodic cross-departmental staff meetings or internal communications designed to inform employees of the importance of the other areas within the organization will help to alleviate an "us versus them" mentality.

The Obligatory Football Analogy

As a football fan and former high school player, Kevin appreciates how all the pieces must come together for success. No matter how good a running back may be, without other players creating a hole, there is no chance of success (unless of course you are the great Barry Sanders). Kevin thinks back to his days as a running back and regrets now that he only focused on his assignment.

Through practice, he knew that if things went as planned a hole was supposed to be there for him to run through. What was never explained to him was what everyone else's roles needed to be in order for that to happen. What would have been the advantage to having that knowledge? Would it have made him a better runner? Probably not, but it would have made him a much better teammate. He would have better understood what it takes to win because he would have learned the importance of the collective roles.

He wonders now if there could have been greater team cohesiveness if the coaches had taken the time to share with the running backs what the linemen were up against in order to create a hole. Can you have a well-oiled machine with totally independent parts? As Duke University basketball coach Mike Krzyzewski says about another sport, "To me, teamwork is the beauty of our sport, where you have five acting as one. You become selfless."

Managers should explain to each employee why his or her role is important and show him or her how that work fits in with other employees to achieve the big-picture vision. This investment of time and effort can pay enormous dividends for your organization.

Tools

Be Positive and Complimentary of Other Employees

It is impressive to customers when you can confidently recommend another employee such as, "I will connect you with Susan Smart; you're going to like her. She will be more than happy to assist you. If you get voice mail, please leave a message and she will get right back to you." But before you can tell customers that a fellow employee will do a great job for them, you first must know and respect that the employee will deliver.

Don't Tolerate Negativism in Front of Customers

An issue surfaced with one of our clients where some very subtle "digs" were directed at a colleague by another employee. If the customer senses an underlying negative tone, it is perhaps symptomatic of a larger issue that goes beyond just a couple of employees.

It is important for such incidences to be shared with management. All employees have a responsibility to improve customer service, especially if that means sharing unfavorable employee interactions that occurred in front of customers. In the name of customer service excellence, make sure your employees know that it is not "snitching."

Conduct Cross-Departmental Staff Meetings

One way for a department or other area of the organization to appreciate the symbiotic relationship they have with another department they have frequent contact with is to periodically conduct cross-departmental staff meetings. Structure agendas that allow employees to share experiences and develop operational efficiencies. At the very least, employees will get to know one another and begin to forge the kind of respect that will be positively perceived by customers.

Chapter 9
Respect

> "We are obliged to respect, defend and maintain the common bonds of union and fellowship that exist among all members of the human race."
>
> —Cicero, Roman author, orator, & politician (106 BC–43 BC)

> "Every human being, of whatever origin, of whatever station, deserves respect. We must each respect others even as we respect ourselves."
>
> —U Thant, Burmese diplomat and Secretary General of the United Nations

Key Levels needed to support the turn on:

1. Communicate a Never-Ending Commitment to Excellence
2. Hire People Who Want to Serve Others
3. Directly and Routinely Observe Employees in Action

Have you noticed how a great number of customer service providers don't say "thank you" anymore? As sad as this may sound, getting a "thank you" for handing over *our* money has become a *turn on*. That's because it is totally unexpected. Respect, or acknowledging the customer's rightful place as the source of the organizations' existence, has become the exception rather than the rule. That's the bad news. The good news is that because it is so rare, respect has now become a competitive advantage!

Home Depot Spray Paint

A woman appearing to be in her late 60s tries to ring up a can of spray paint through a Home Depot self-service scanner and it won't work. She tries again and again and finally steps back in frustration. The cashier who is monitoring the scanners yells from about 15 feet away, "What's your birth date?"

"What do you need to know that for?" the woman said in an agitated voice. The cashier then explained that the reason the spray paint wasn't ringing up was because it was considered a controlled substance. The customer's birth date unlocked the item, but the cashier had to upset the customer before this information was revealed.

Where was the training on how to handle controlled substances at the scanner so that customers don't get frustrated? But more than that, where was the basic respect afforded seniors who, as most people know, aren't crazy about giving their age, let alone through a public announcement?

"O" Tickets

A couple of years ago, we took our boys to Las Vegas for spring break. We had arranged to see Cirque du Soleil's *Mystere* at Treasure Island and stood in line to pick up our tickets at Will Call. Brooke asked if there were any tickets available during our stay for Cirque du Soleil's "O," which was playing at the Bellagio. In a very condescending voice the ticket person said, "It is sold out." Brooke said, "Well, we're going to be here all week."

"It is sold out until May," the ticket person responded scornfully.

The ticket person failed to add, "You idiot," but it was implied. Okay, she gets asked this question 500 times a day. But what an opportunity to say, "I'm sorry, but it is a very popular show. We don't have anything available while you are here on this visit, but if you call a couple of months in advance, we would love to have you return. You really don't want to miss it!"

While we are not huge fans of detailed scripting—telling employees what they must say can appear stiff to the customer, stifles creativity, and does not influence *how* the message is delivered—we do advocate scripts for frequently asked questions. Staff should be trained to create positive messages for common questions such as a sold-out show so that all they have to remember is to smile and be pleasant.

Prior to this brief encounter, we had high regard for Cirque du Soleil. In about two seconds, this ticket person managed to denigrate that perception. Selling the product shouldn't stop because you don't happen to *need* customers that day! High demand is never an excuse for rudeness. Businesses that are on top today can quickly find themselves on the bottom tomorrow.

Everyone in the organization must maintain the high standards that were so painstakingly achieved; that includes selling tickets. The ticket person and a concession stand employee were the only people in the Cirque du Soleil organization with whom we came in direct contact at the show. Why spend the unbelievable time, talent, and money required to attract us to the show, only to have a ticket person push us away?

Friend of the Company

Consider how you treat the ones you love. You enjoy sharing things important to you. You tell them things you wouldn't tell anyone else. Your love for them and the moments you share are at the center of your relationship.

In the hierarchy of human relationships, let's assume you would prioritize your relationships in the following manner: 1) spouse or significant other, 2) friends, 3) relatives, 4) co-workers, and 5) strangers.

The choice of your spouse as the first priority is obvious. Your friends would likely be a second priority, because you choose to care for them. Relatives could be interchanged with friends, but for the sake of argument, let's call it a close third. You didn't choose them but you still love them. Next are the people you work with. The bond is the shared experience. You are all in it together. In fact, our mystery shopping research in 2005 has shown that 95% of employees were perceived as having respect for other employees, but only 90% of the evaluated employees showed respect for customers.

Needless to say, bringing up the rear as the last priority would be the people you do not know. Which brings us to the question, where would you place customers in this list? Closer to strangers than friends? We contend that in most organizations, especially those where the sheer volume of business makes the names and faces of customer's unrecognizable, customers are treated as last priority because they are seen as strangers. There is no emotional connection. And where there is no emotional connection, there can be no respect.

What if you could convince employees that customers are friends? By accepting the job, haven't employees essentially agreed to treat each customer like a "friend of the company"? Think of each employee as a greeter at a fundraising party the organization is throwing for its patrons. The greeter may not know everyone personally, but he makes the best impression by genuinely welcoming the guests, introducing himself, and setting the tone for a pleasurable evening by making them aware of where everything can be found.

The organization should go to all this effort for three important reasons:

1. You want everyone to feel comfortable with the surroundings.
2. The patrons have shown their true support for what you are doing by attending.
3. They are going to hand you a big check at the end of the evening.

The greeter does not have to be coerced into acting a certain way because he understands the purpose of the fundraiser. He knows how to treat patrons and he also knows that the end result will mean more revenue, benefiting everyone in the organization.

There is a debate in our office over the following statement: "If an employee is happy at work, they will pass that happiness on to the customer." We always take the position, based on years of consulting experience and thousands of mystery shops, that employee satisfaction and customer satisfaction are not directly related. We have seen too many instances of "happy" employees becoming complacent with customers. For example, a mystery shopper who poses as a mother calls Emergency Services because her child has been struck by a car. She is told, "Hang on a sec, I will help you after I finish something." The staff person then sets the receiver down—without putting the call on hold—so that she can fix her printer.

Organizations must never shift away from customer satisfaction to focus on employee satisfaction as if the two are mutually exclusive.

The Invisible Customer

An employee of ours told us a story of how she stood at a counter unacknowledged for several minutes in full view of employees and how this made her feel "invisible." Not that this is new; we have all experienced this inexplicable event. However, it brought to mind the fact that many businesses today do not seem to understand the ramifications of making us feel invisible.

What happens if we continue to go to a place where we are made to feel invisible? First of all, shame on us because we have been conditioned to accept poor customer service. But what if there is no alternative or it is not convenient for us to seek an alternative at that moment? The first thing it does is give the organization a false sense of security; that is, our satisfaction scores aren't so good, but the bottom line is great. How long can that last?

The second thing is that it creates anti-marketing. Customers may not possess the conviction to make a change, but they will certainly voice anger and frustration to others. So in effect, while we are paying an organization for a product or service, we are working against them. Any company that sees that as a fair trade will never be successful.

The notion that customers feel invisible is a cultural phenomenon in that the organization allows it to exist either consciously or subconsciously. Some managers may truly see it as a fair exchange because they are negatively affected by factors such as a lack of skilled service providers or high turnover. However, it is our belief that most managers turn a blind eye to the attention employees pay to customers simply out of laziness.

Our mystery shopping research over the past eight years would indicate that managers are assuming way too much if they believe employees (even happy ones) will inherently respect customers.

Respecting Customers on the Telephone

Employees often do not give telephone communication the same degree of attention as in-person encounters. However, the same opportunities for excellent customer service that exist when someone is standing in front of an employee are the same ones available on the telephone. *Customers* are not paying any less attention to how they are respected when they are on the telephone.

Positive telephone experiences are essential to an overall customer service strategy because the positive behavior conveyed invites the caller into a relationship. Extra effort entices the caller to choose the company, and a pleasant experience serves to positively represent the entire organization.

When things happen too fast for a customer because the employee spoke too quickly or he or she gave the customer the impression that they were in a hurry to end the call, it sends the message that the call is not important. The customer feels rushed off the line without a sense of closure.

There are a number of fundamental customer service skills that should take place in the first five to ten seconds of a telephone encounter. The customer service standards utilized by most of our studies evaluate a number of these skills, such as answering the telephone within three rings, identifying oneself and one's place of business, and asking how to help the customer.

How one delivers these skills is just as essential. If the introduction is delivered too fast, or spoken with a harsh tone of voice, or if the customer is left on hold too long (especially with dead air), it unnecessarily irritates the customer and then requires a special effort to bring the relationship back. This would not be necessary if the little things that should be done routinely were accomplished in the first place.

Tools

How to Handle "Stupid" Customers

We acknowledge that some customers may test an employee's patience, but nothing positive for the employee or the organization can ever come from showing displeasure. Here are some steps to follow when confronted by such a situation:

- Avoid judging the customer. Remember the opening quote from U Thant, former Secretary General of the United Nations, "Every human being, of whatever origin, of whatever station, deserves respect. We must each respect others even as we respect ourselves."
- Avoid showing frustration. Customers will take frustration as a sign that the employee thinks they are not very bright. This will lead to a negative reaction and potential loss of the customer.
- Clarify the facts. Seek as much detail as possible to better understand the customer's need.
- Express a desire to help. State your interest in assisting the customer and commit to getting answers.
- Stay with the customer. Employees should do everything they can to avoid passing the customer off to another employee in an effort to make it someone else's problem.
- Verify that they understand. Once the issue has been resolved, make sure the customer is clear on the information.

How to Manage Difficult Customers

We prefer the word managing to the word handling because it has a more positive connotation in that it suggests a level of skill on the employee's part. The following are some suggestions for managing difficult customers:

- Don't take it personally.
- Listen to identify central ideas and specific facts.
- Take notes.
- Eliminate distractions.
- Acknowledge concerns at the beginning.
- Avoid words such as "okay," "but," or "however."
- Apologize for the inconvenience they experienced.
- Paraphrase what you have heard.
- Be flexible on policies.
- Offer alternatives.

Learn from the Experience

Having a strategy for learning from experiences with difficult people will serve to make future experiences more manageable. Follow these steps after such experiences:

- Ask a supervisor to join you to be a part of the transaction.
- Debrief the situation with someone else after the customer leaves (in a secure location).
- Learn stress techniques to stay calm. Breathe deeply and focus on the positives.
- Recognize that customers will have bad days; it is not personal!
- Consider what you would do differently next time.

Chapter 10

Friendliness

> "A cheerful look brings joy to the heart, and good news brings health to the heart."
>
> —Proverbs 15:30

Key Levels needed to support the turn on:

2. Hire People Who Want to Serve Others
5. Establish Accountability for Frontline Success

Because most customer service situations involve two strangers interacting for a matter of minutes, friendliness is the quickest and often the only way to convey a positive message to customers. It is a *turn on* for customers because it makes them feel good, it gives them hope that a relationship is possible, and it gives them one less stressful thing to worry about in their lives.

Many customers take an employee's friendliness toward them as a personal connection. It is usually all customers have to go on. In their minds, customers believe they deserve something for their patronage and that starts with a friendly staff. But instead of focusing on this critically important *turn on*, the simplicity of being nice to customers is too often taken for granted by organizations.

Many organizations mistakenly assume that customer service excellence must come at a higher price. As a result, they roll out complicated programs when all they need to do is to convince their employees to be nicer. Most organizations don't emphasize friendliness with their employees because they assume it's such a basic and obvious quality that employees will naturally do it.

Therefore, the key to success is not convincing employees to be nice to everyone, but training them on how to *appear* to be nice even when they don't feel like it. The message to employees must be, "The goal is to be friendly every single time. Now, let's work on how you get there."

Customers don't care about genuine, they care about the appearance of genuine. Usually in the time allotted to serve someone, they aren't questioning sincerity (although sincerity is preferred). Everyone would be more than happy to do business with people who can at least fake liking us.

Customer Service Acting 101

As organizations struggle with the erosion of customer service, they must focus more on customer perceptions. What do we, as a customer, want from a customer service provider? We want friendliness, competence, and a passion for what they have chosen to do. We also expect employees to be the best their company has to offer, because our perception of the company and any future business we do with them rests on it.

As customers, it is important to realize that our perception of a transaction is the correct impression. In other words, if an employee appears rude to us, it doesn't matter (and in fact we're unlikely to know) if he was *unintentionally* rude. Likewise, if an employee appears to be friendly, that's good enough for us. As customers, we're unlikely to push that relationship by asking the friendly employee if he'd like to come over to watch the ballgame on Saturday with our other friends.

As customer service providers, we need to move away from a "just be yourself" service philosophy. Too many employees are just being themselves, which is why customers have so many bad experiences. We need to teach employees how to be someone else. Don't put your employees through customer service training; instead, put them through an acting class.

The primary goal of putting employees through Customer Service Acting 101 is to teach them how easy it is for "life to imitate art." We start by letting them know that for the four, six, or eight hours they work, they are free to be someone else, preferably someone who likes people, in order to give customers what they really want.

Next we teach them to smile, rather than telling them it is their job to smile. Have them practice being more animated and polite. Take it a step further by having them put on nametags or dressing up as actors and actresses they admire.

When they are ready to begin serving customers, you may want to have them wear dual nametags—their own and their alter egos. This may cause customers to ask questions and reinforce the positive training experience through the additional attention they receive.

Here are five guidelines for implementing Customer Service Acting 101:

1. Make it a policy that all employees must go through Customer Service Acting 101 before they can begin serving customers.
2. Make it fun, but take preparation of the class seriously.
3. Help employees learn coping and recovery skills by role-playing, where they deal with difficult customers and common mistakes.
4. Test what your actors have learned on real customers. Have employees serve customers as themselves and then as their new alter ego to find out which personality is better received by customers.
5. Keep their "acting careers" alive by conducting periodic refresher courses.

Mandated Friendliness

A "Miss Manners" column appeared in the newspaper some years back commenting indirectly on issues related to Safeway grocery stores' mandated friendliness policy. The policy had resulted in a lawsuit by a female employee that charged the organization with causing sexual advances. Apparently she experienced or believed that overt friendliness was perceived as a come-on by male customers. In response to the policy, Miss Manners wrote, "Policies requiring employees to provide friendly service are designed to stamp out prevailing policies that permit surly service... But Be Friendly Or Else never works because both the problem and the solution are based on failure to understand the situation."

Miss Manners highlighted a 12-step process that explained how policies of this kind work until they eventually go full circle:

1. Someone in a public service industry notices that the public doesn't like being treated rudely.
2. Employees are told that they are now required to engage customers in friendly chatter.
3. Employees protest that the policy is a waste of time and money, that it adds another burden to their work.
4. It becomes apparent that the friendliness policy can only be enforced by policing the employees.
5. The customers complain that the friendliness seems forced.
6. Someone in management notices that the employees are wasting time and money chatting.
7. Some customers denounce the friendliness as intrusive while other customers return the friendliness in ways that the employees find intrusive.
8. Someone in management notices that management's time is being wasted trying to placate all those whom friendliness has made disgruntled.
9. The policy is dropped.
10. The customers complain that the employees are surly.
11. Time passes, and eventually someone else comes up with the idea of requiring employees to act friendly.
12. Reprise 2 through 11.

We understand and appreciate what Safeway had in mind. In fact, we like the idea of mandatory friendliness a great deal. The problem seems to be that the organization had not positioned itself so that the policy was comfortable and acceptable to both customers and employees. What training was involved in helping employees understand what their parameters were? Were various role-playing scenarios created to help make their efforts more natural? Reinforcing the policy in this manner would have avoided Miss Manners' Step #5, "The customers complain that the friendliness seems forced," and perhaps broken the 12-step cycle.

The main issue is not about following friendliness procedures; it is about the perception left with the customer.

Dental Desertion

We recently took on a client who had just opened a dental practice. Normally we don't work with small businesses, but the practice was only about 10 miles from our office, so we could use our local office staff for the mystery shopping component of the consulting project.

The mystery shopping scenario was a simple one: sign up as a new patient and evaluate all that entails.

Our staff found the dental practice extremely friendly and exceedingly thorough. They uniformly felt that staff answered the telephone professionally, with a warm tone, and a genuine desire to help. The staff also set up appointments to fit the client's schedule, not just the next available appointment. They explained everything that would happen on the first visit and for the patient's convenience mailed the paperwork ahead of time so they wouldn't have to do it all when they arrived.

When patients arrived, the office staff greeted them and asked if they would like a cup of coffee. Shoppers were given a full tour of the office including meeting all the staff. Even the other dentist popped out to meet one shopper. However, the quintessential moment for one shopper was being asked what television station she wanted to watch while getting her teeth cleaned.

The whole dental experience was so good that everyone who shopped the practice became patients, including our family.

This, of course, meant leaving our previous dentist, but the positive experience we had at the new dentist served to highlight the unhappiness with our previous dentist that we had been sharing with one another for some time. The issue was clearly one of customer service and not dental care. In fact, the new dentist couldn't say enough about the quality of the dental work we had been receiving. This was reassuring, but as customers, we still felt unhappy at our previous dentist. Staff turnover at that practice, in the midst of the dentist's attempt to provide higher-end dental work, left gaping holes in customer service that caused us to feel unappreciated.

Our previous dentist had lost sight of one of the golden rules of small business: Always make sure your existing customers are covered during your hot pursuit of more business. In violation of this rule, he made less time for his "regular" customers. To make matters worse, he did not seem to realize that the new frontline employees hired were not friendly. They made little effort to overcome their newness with increased effort. The little customer service touches the practice once had were gone. As much as most people dread going to the dentist, it is at least the quality of care or caring that can make it tolerable.

The process we went through in switching dentists reflects how most customers approach change. But while an organization goes through changes that are either intentional (expanding) or unintentional (turnover), they must be mindful of the fact that customers are evaluating what that change means to them. Is the business still a good fit for them?

What could our previous dentist have done to keep his customers? One *turn on* would have been to hire frontline people who already had a strong sense of customer service and then train them on details that are important to his patients. A warm greeting and a pleasant tone of voice on the telephone are an excellent start.

He could have his staff introduce themselves to patients and share a little bit about themselves and what they hoped to accomplish in the job. Confidence and pride in one's work is always an effective way to build new relationships.

Finally, he could take the opportunity to get patient feedback on the current state of his practice so that he could quickly address any concerns. Along that same line, he could conduct an exit survey to understand why customers stopped making appointments; without this tool, it is unlikely he will realize that he's losing patients over poor customer service. Organizations in this position are likely to suffer substantial financial loss as they continue losing customers.

"Hi," Staples Style

In the particular Staples store we frequent, there is a cash register that also serves as a return desk to the customer's left as they enter the store. One day as Brooke was approaching this register she heard the clerk say "Hi" to a customer entering the store. Unfortunately, by the time the customer heard it, it was being directed to the back of the customer's head. When Brooke reached the clerk, she said, "I couldn't help but hear you say 'Hi' to a customer walking through the door, is that something you do on your own?" "Yes," she said. "You mean no one asked you to do that?" Brooke asked. "Well, yeah," she said, "They said if I didn't do it, they would fire me." She got even more animated and said with obvious frustration, "And I'm the only one who has to do it. They must be trying to get rid of me!"

There are two issues at play here, and both suggest the employee was right to be upset. First, if you were the employee, would you feel singled out if management had bothered to explain why it was important for you to greet each customer? Would you still see saying "hello" to customers as punitive? Of course, it depends on the rationality of the explanation; which brings us to the second point, is saying hello to customers in this fashion good customer service? We originally indicated where this employee was stationed for a reason. Nine times out of ten she was delivering her greeting to the backs of the customers. As a result, it became an impersonal gesture, and it was therefore seen by customers as a mandatory salutation.

"Hi," Blockbuster Style

A shopper entered a Blockbuster and before he was two feet inside the door, he heard someone yell, "Hi." It wasn't a personal, eye contact greeting, so he looked around not sure whom it was directed at. Behind the counter was an employee, but she wasn't looking in his direction. The shopper surmised that this was their new way of "getting close" to the customer.

We are not fans of one-size-fits-all customer service. We dislike it when gimmicks are chosen in lieu of encouraging great individual service. Are we really supposed to enjoy someone forcing out a greeting simply because we have opened the front door?

Let's look at what happened at the end of the shopper's visit to Blockbuster. There were five employees visible as he stood in line with his DVDs. Only two were assisting customers as the line began to grow and stretch to the back of the store. In plain view of everyone, an employee, who has not been assisting customers, picks up the telephone. When she finally hangs up, she chats with another employee for a few seconds and then leaves. Is it possible that she doesn't see the line weaving its way to back of the store? Does she not care? Does she have a different responsibility than the other employees? Perhaps, but customers don't care about any of that. They don't want to stand in line at the store holding their movies; they want to be at home watching their movies.

Have you ever thought about what employees may be saying to one another when they sense a customer's impatience? In this instance, it might go something like this: "Who does that customer think he is? We've got a hundred customers here, and we have to get all these DVDs and videos back on the shelves. Somebody has to answer the phone. I'd like to see him do this work all day. At least he gets to go home and relax. Give me a break!"

Who is at fault? The problem lies with Blockbuster. It is a faulty process that puts non-customer-related functions in front of waiting customers. They should move the telephone to a back office and also consider moving returned rentals as well. Instead of merely saying a phony hello to customers, put the effort into making the checkout process run more smoothly and efficiently. That gives a better impression of trying.

"Hi," Kinkos Style

The cash register at the local Kinkos sits on a counter to the right a few paces from the front door. They designed it to face the direction of the front door. As Brooke walked in one day, she noticed something completely new. The employee behind the counter looked directly at her and said, "Hello." Mindful that greeting customers is a trend in retail, her sense was that this gesture was natural. It had the desired effect because she genuinely liked it.

We have three examples of a similar action performed in the name of good customer service: one that made the customer feel welcome, and two that left the customer uncomfortable. Obviously the problem is not the gesture; it is the lack of sincerity and direct eye contact. At Kinkos, Brooke felt the warmth and sincerity of the greeter who was facing the entrance to the store. At Blockbuster and Staples, customers were given only an obligatory greeting to the back of the head.

Tools

Create a Friendlier Culture

There are a number of things organizations can do to create a friendlier culture:

- Instruct employees on the importance of all customers to the organization.
- Interview employees who have been observed as unfriendly to understand their source of unhappiness and present them with alternatives.
- Observe employees in action with customers.
- Instruct employees that rudeness will be disciplined.
- Evaluate whether or not the right employees are dealing with customers.

Show Customers Little Kindnesses

One mystery shopper put it in perspective by attributing a positive encounter to "little kindnesses" of empathy, compassion, and warmth. Encourage employees that it is as much about their personal touch as it is the information provided that makes for a satisfying experience.

Chapter 11
Matching the Customer's Pace

> "The best salespeople see things through their customers' eyes, modify their styles to their customers' chemistry, and pull together their offering to meet their customers' needs."
>
> —Beth Klein, President & CEO,
> GE Medical Systems

Key Levels needed to support the turn on:

3. Directly and Routinely Observe Employees in Action
4. Utilize Coaching Techniques
5. Establish Accountability for Frontline Success

Perhaps most people are more patient than we are, but we find employees who seem to have just one speed—annoying. They are not enough in tune with customers to move from their self-imposed pace to match the customers'. Great customer service providers are like race cars. They use multiple speeds depending on whatever the challenges are on the course. They can downshift to address more demanding customers or go full throttle if that is what the customer demands.

It is a *turn on* when employees react to customer cues and match the pace at which the customer wants to conclude a transaction. However, for it to be a memorable experience the customer must recognize that the employee is making an intentional effort. Words can serve as the bridge between the customer's desire and the action that will achieve that desire. Contrast a man who is constantly looking at his watch with a woman who wants to know what an employee thinks about the news of the day. The impatient "watch looker" might respond well to an employee saying something unsolicited like, "I'm going to have you out of here as soon as possible" and then visibly accelerate the transaction. For the customer who likes to chat, the employee should be prepared to downshift to small talk. However, chatty customers will not be turned on unless they perceive that the employee is showing a genuine interest.

The goal is to address whatever situation may be at hand and "play" to the customer's desire at the speed that is required. In addition, employees should always be conscious of the customer's time while always looking for ways to streamline the experience.

Acknowledgment Is Critical

The time that lapses between the customer's decision to engage and the employee's acknowledgment is critical. With each second that passes, customers lose confidence in their decision to engage, which can take them from positive expectations, to uncertainty, to insecurity, to discomfort, to frustration, and finally to anger in a very short period of time. Although an employee may take less than a minute to acknowledge a customer, those seconds seem like an eternity to the person waiting. Needless to say, this is no way to start a relationship.

New customers, in particular, are not familiar with the company's processes and procedures. When they are not acknowledged immediately, they feel awkward and "invisible," which may feel like a slap in the face. When this happens with regularity, it signals that serving customers is not a priority for the organization.

One of our workshop exercises involves role-playing a scenario in which one person acts as a waiting customer while a second person, acting as the employee, finds ways to ignore the "customer" for 20 seconds. Everyone who participates is amazed at how long 20 seconds seems.

This exercise provides a better perspective on the customer's view of time, but nothing beats direct observation of the way employees acknowledge customers.

In *You've Only Got Three Seconds*, Camille Livingston says, "The real world has your number. It only takes three seconds to know where you're coming from." If that is in fact the speed of perception, then employees need to be mindful that customers will take only three seconds to make a judgment about the employee and the level of customer service they're giving. Work with individual employees on the speed of their acknowledgment so that they are not judged unfairly.

Debit or Credit?

A shopper was mailing a package through the United States Postal Service. The person at the counter told him the cost would be $3.95. He handed the clerk a $20 bill. The USPS employee asked, "Would you like to use a debit card or a credit card?" "No," the shopper said, "I already handed you cash. Why would you ask me that if I just handed you cash?" "We are required to ask that or they mark us down," the postal worker explained. "Actually," the postal worker confessed, "it is easier for us. The machine adds up the receipts; otherwise we have to add up the cash at the end of the day."

When managers hand down mandates like this to employees, it must be explained within the framework of great customer service. To insult customers or waste their time with something that is not for their convenience is counterproductive. One cannot expect employees to show the proper amount of flexibility if no fundamental guidelines have been established first. For example, as obvious as it may seem, someone needed to tell the postal worker, "You are only allowed to ask the debit or credit question before the transaction has occurred or if the customer has a card in his or her hand." Otherwise, some employees will surprisingly attempt to implement rules without any thought to how offensive or inappropriate they may appear to customers. In this instance, pace is being used in reverse, with the customer being asked to care about the time associated with USPS operations.

Don't Make Your Life Part of My Life, Please!

A shopper went to Pizza Hut and ordered the salad bar. The waitress explained that the salad bar wasn't set up because the person responsible got drunk the night before and had to call in sick. This explanation clearly fell under the "too much information" category. An extreme example, to be sure, but the point is that customers know what they want from employees—and it doesn't include personal exploits or dirty laundry. Nothing is less professional.

Even more common is being an unwitting party to co-workers talking out loud to one another, in the presence of customers, about their daily lives. Employees should be coached that all personal conversations stop immediately in the presence of customers. In fact, if the organization adheres to the "I'm ready when you are" concept discussed in Chapter 1, communication should stop *before* the customer is in the employee's presence.

Tools

Identify the Customer's Pace

- Listen for verbal cues. The customer's speech pattern and choice of words will tell an employee if the customer will gain more satisfaction out of talking or leaving.
- Be aware of non-verbal cues. A customer's body language will signal his or her patience with the pace of the experience.
- Respect the customer's time. Employees should always be conscious of the customer's time while always looking for ways to streamline the experience.

Develop a Process for Addressing Service Delays

- Always explain to customers ahead of time why a delay is going to occur.
- Whenever possible, let the customer know who will be assisting them and approximately how long it will be.
- Discuss with staff dialogue that is appropriate during a delay. What would you like to hear when you are waiting in a line or in a waiting room?
- Role-play situations that could occur while someone is waiting, that is, other people being helped, and discuss how these situations could be prevented.
- What measures could be taken to make up for the customer's inconvenience?
- Always apologize for any wait regardless of the duration.

Explore More Effective Ways to Address Acknowledging the Customer Immediately

- Use an egg timer to demonstrate the passage of time, especially from the customer's perspective.
- For one weekend, have employees measure time in relation to the customer service they receive in the "real world," that is, time in line, time waiting for assistance, and so on.
- Make direct contact with the customer mandatory, that is, no greetings from cubicles.
- Practice the "one second rule." Making eye contact with the customer and holding up the index finger—the symbol for "I will be with you in a second"—will diffuse customer frustration as long as it becomes a reality.
- Make an employee the primary greeter. Instruct them that greeting customers is more important than any other responsibilities.

Chapter 12
Recognizing Customers

> "There are two things people want more than sex and money…recognition and praise."
>
> —Mary Kay Ash

Key Levels needed to support the turn on:

1. Communicate a Never-Ending Commitment to Excellence
4. Utilize Coaching Techniques

When customers visit your organization, you don't want them walking away humming the Foreigner song "Feels Like the First Time." Unlike the song, this persistent state of anonymity is not a positive thing with most customers.

Being recognized as a customer is an instant *turn on*. It is natural for people to gravitate to organizations that make the effort to remember them. But unless you live in a town of 100 people, remembering customers is a difficult thing to do. It takes a concerted effort and some skill, but the return on this small investment is immeasurable.

The golf season in Indiana is typically eight or nine months long, although diehards do their best to stretch it. In late March, The Fort Golf Course and Resort in Indianapolis opened for the season, and using the excuse of an unseasonably warm day, Kevin grabbed his clubs to play nine holes. As he entered the clubhouse, he was immediately recognized with a smile by Donnie, the assistant pro. "Hi, Kevin," he said as they shook hands, "good to see you again."

Kevin plays a fair number of rounds at The Fort each year, but he did not expect someone he had only known casually for a year to remember him by name after the winter layoff. With this little gesture, Kevin instantly got a sense of belonging and acceptance.

Do You Know Me?

Have you ever tried to get a business to remember you? We are reminded of the American Express commercial "Do you know me?" every time we think a company should recognize us for our contribution to their success. Unfortunately, they rarely do.

A few years back we thought it might be fun to be a "regular" at some restaurant. We were looking for a *Cheers*-like experience. We envisioned walking through the door, having the host beam at seeing us, and shake our hands as he showed us to our favorite table. He would then ask us if our drink order was the "usual."

So one night, we decided we were going to work on our strategy. We asked the waitress to make a special attempt to remember us and where we were sitting. We all had a good laugh. The next time we were in the restaurant we discovered that it had been sold and the staff had a massive turnover. It seems we were destined to dine in obscurity.

The act of recognizing customers sends multiple messages. First, it tells them that they are valued. Regular customers inherently know you need them, but they need to know that the organization appreciates that fact. Another message being sent to customers is that the organization is seeking to build a relationship. It's human nature for customers to want to do business with organizations that clearly make an effort to recognize them.

Customers Aren't Strangers

Customers become very annoyed when they are treated like strangers by customer service providers. Strangers are someone you have absolutely no vested interest in. They walk by and you don't care one way or another about them. There's no history and no relationship, and you don't desire one. Customers should be the people that service providers are immediately attracted to and want to get to know better, as in, "If I can get to know that person better, something great may come of this."

So customers ask themselves, why do we feel like we are not essential to service providers? Too often customers are put in the awkward position of thanking *employees* either because they were able to give correct change back, or simply to fill the void of silence.

We sometimes like to use the term "love" in reference to customer service, as in, "I'm not feeling the love." It is used for effect, but in a very real way, we want the places we go to day in and day out to appreciate what we mean to them and to show their appreciation.

Many customers suspect that they probably shouldn't care too much, but receiving bad service personally offends them. This feeling is aggravated when employees fail to recognize the face of a customer who frequents their business. In person the business treats the customer like a stranger, yet the business has a sophisticated database somewhere that knows the customer exists, because he or she gets junk mail and e-mails that prove it. It seems that with all the computer databases out there, organizations are more interested in buying habits than customer relationships!

The Ultimate Driving Machine

A couple of years ago we decided we were ready to own the "Ultimate Driving Machine" and bought a used BMW 5-series. When we first contacted the local dealership for servicing, they were very impressive. A service representative we will call John was assigned to us. So far, so good. Having one individual you can go to who knows you and knows your car is as good as it gets.

Unfortunately, as time went along and we realized we had purchased a lemon, our frustration was exacerbated by the fact that John didn't know who we were from one visit to the next. He also didn't seem to recall what was wrong with our car even though we had been to the dealership four times in two months for the same problem. We often wondered what the computer on John's desk was for if it wasn't able to give him a maintenance history of our car's servicing.

We finally took the service manager aside to explain that John may be the determining factor as to whether we buy another BMW and that a change in service representative may be in order. After all, what is the point of having your own personal service representative if there is nothing personal about the experience? It seems the dealership wanted to get us, but didn't want to put forth the effort to keep us.

The postscript is that we have since purchased a new BMW, and our dealership has dropped the "big city" arrogance and has treated us with respect. Too bad we had to travel 40 miles to another town to get it. But sometimes that is what customers do when expectations go unmet.

Dave Belanger

Dave Belanger is a marvel. He's the kind of person you tell everyone about. Dave has moved on to bigger and better things, but he was once the locker room attendant at Sycamore Hills Golf Club, an upscale, private club in Fort Wayne, Indiana, where he set out to make every member and guest feel like a million bucks.

From the first time Kevin set foot in Dave's locker room, he remembered Kevin with a polite, "Good afternoon, Mr. Billingsley. How are you today?" *Mister* Billingsley? The first time he said that, Kevin was in his 30s and hardly feeling like a mister. Mind you, Kevin only played the course at Sycamore Hills two or three times a year as a guest or in an outing. But every time he got the chance, Dave was there with the same respectful salutation.

The true proof of Dave's skill at recognition was the night he offered a "Hi, Mr. Billingsley" to Kevin while at a hockey game. Kevin knew immediately he should recognize this guy who was greeting him but failed to make the connection. Dave extended a hand and introduced himself, seemingly taking some pleasure in the fact that he was putting Kevin at a disadvantage.

Should Kevin have cared whether or not Dave Belanger had a system, had taken a class to achieve this ability, or was just naturally good at recalling names? Should he have cared that Dave was too polite or that his wide-eyed exuberance was just an act? Of course not. All that really mattered to Kevin, as a customer, was his positive perception of Sycamore Hills Golf Club, which was embodied in the spirit of this outstanding employee. The impression was that, even as a guest, this club must have thought Kevin was worthy of special attention because they hired a professional like Dave.

Kevin was so overwhelmed with Dave's ability to provide extraordinary customer service that he interviewed him. The fact is Dave cared enough to actually have a system. He used association by mentally recording who came with whom and for what event. He would also refer to a list of everyone that was expected to play that day. That he was able to put this skill to incredible use and that he remembered Kevin at the hockey game was just a touch of class. Not every business has the luxury of knowing which customers will walk in that day. For those that do, requiring that employees look over the list is an excellent start to recognizing the customer.

Why Not Use What You Know About Customers?

Several grocery stores in our area, most notably Kroger, have member discount cards. Every time, without fail, their employees ask if we have our Kroger cards. Their consistency is admirable. But why does it have to stop there? Doesn't the card signify that we are known and loyal customers? Here is a rarely taken opportunity to tell customers how much they appreciate them. This can be accomplished effectively by using customer names and thanking them for their continued business.

While a customer may be a stranger to an employee, the organization is not a stranger to the customer. This is why it is important to put customer information in the hands of frontline employees whenever possible. How important is it for your pharmacy to have a record of your medications in its computer? When you show up, they can tell in seconds what your history is with them and be in a position to provide valuable health advice. Wouldn't it be nice if they also used your name?

When it is not possible to go to a database (or, like the Sycamore Hills Golf Club, consult a list of customers that are expected to walk through the door that day), employees should be trained to gently probe for historical information. It may be a question as simple as, "Have you been with us before? How was your last experience?" Employees must then be ready to address whatever concerns the customer reveals.

Brooke has always wondered why she doesn't get an e-mail from a local office supply store thanking her for her business. She has been a loyal customer for years and presents a store credit card and a cash-back program card when she makes purchases. Wouldn't you think that would trigger that she is someone important to them? Perhaps her loyalty means something to the corporate folks, but it is never acknowledged by the person behind the register.

While Brooke does like receiving the cash-back checks in the mail, it's not like having them send a note saying, "Brooke, we see you bought a printer from us today. We realize you could have gone to a lot of other places, but you chose us instead. Thanks!" They have all the information they could ever want on her purchasing history. Why not put the technology to work and personalize it?

Tools

Tips on Recognizing Customers

- Work at remembering frequent customers. Remember names, study faces, and mentally record what their relationship is with your organization.
- Make every attempt to use the customer's name based on whatever information they provide to you, such as credit cards, product returns, or applications. For instance, a "Thank you

Mrs. Billingsley" when a credit card slip is returned rarely goes unnoticed.
- Employees can't remember everyone, but there are ways to give the perception of recognizing customers. The simplest is to give all customers a look of recognition whether you think you have seen them before or not. A smile and a friendly hello can signal that you are glad to see them *again*.

Chapter 13
Being Proactive

> "Opportunity is missed by most because it is dressed in overalls and looks like work."
>
> —Thomas Edison

Key Levels needed to support the turn on:

2. Hire People Who Want to Serve Others
3. Directly and Routinely Observe Employees in Action
4. Utilize Coaching Techniques
5. Establish Accountability for Frontline Success

By offering additional solutions or accommodating special requests, proactive employees create a favorable impression of the organization. It is a *turn on* when employees aggressively act on behalf of the customer and look for opportunities to exceed expectations.

"Call to tell us you're coming."

We have noticed a trend by some organizations that rely on customer appointments. The organization calls and leaves a message during the day to remind the customer of a future appointment. The organization then demands that the customer call back to confirm the appointment.

We think this may be setting a bad precedent. We know that it costs the organization money when customers fail to show up for appointments. However, many of these organizations already charge customers in that situation. So why do the organizations make their loyal customers jump through more hoops just because of a few deadbeats?

Instead of tailoring their efforts based on a customer's past history, or giving a newcomer the benefit of the doubt, these organizations apply a "one-size-fits-all" rule. This is offensive and a waste of time for the customers who take their appointments seriously; most consumers will say they refuse to be treated as the lowest common denominator.

Speaking Well of Other Employees

Customers respond to employees who tell them how good another employee is. Customers appreciate stepping into an environment where the team members proactively know and support one another. Who wouldn't feel good about the following referral from a florist?

"You really need to talk to Randy because he is the best landscaper in town. He's fun to work with, and he'll make your house look like a million bucks."

Would you seek out Randy for your landscaping? Of course you would. There is every reason to believe Randy is great because you presume the person doing the referring is a reliable source since she sounds like she has worked with Randy.

We are definitely not suggesting that employees "talk up" staff when they don't know that person or aren't familiar enough with the customer's needs. For example, what value would the referral be if the referrer is promoting Randy because he is an unemployed second cousin? Cross-selling the organization's products or services can be very effective, but only when employees know firsthand the people they are referring the customer to, and only when the recommendation is genuinely in the customer's best interest.

Just such an experience occurred recently when a shopper made a call to a hospital's outpatient registration area of behalf of her young son. The call was answered by Dawn, and after an exchange of patient information, she had several helpful suggestions for the shopper's son, including:

1. Be sure to tell your son about the trip to the lab a couple days in advance.
2. Explain to him that in order to play baseball, this must be done.
3. Call ahead and pre-register him so you can come right in after you pick him up from school.
4. Call the lab on the day you are coming, and they will try to place him in a room right away so he doesn't have to wait around and become more anxious.
5. Tell him they have "really good blood drawers here who use small needles."

At the conclusion of the conversation, Dawn said she had a ten-year-old son herself and reiterated her advice and said that these tactics had worked well with her own son, who had to undergo medical tests and procedures recently.

Dawn mentioned that all their phlebotomists are good with kids and some are really excellent. She told the shopper that if she brought her son in after 4:00 p.m. next week, she would leave a note for Jared, who is really excellent with children. She added that it might help to have a man draw his blood.

The employee not only made a personal connection with the shopper, but she selected the one phlebotomist she knew from experience would do the best job.

Olive Garden Survey

Two shoppers ate dinner at an Olive Garden restaurant. Unfortunately on this night, the customer service was inconsistent. The server finally explained during the meal that he was new. His defense of his newness bordered on annoying when he told the shoppers that they had been randomly picked for a survey and that it would mean a discount off their next meal. He then said that someone was coming by the table to take care of it.

The shoppers assumed this person, presumably a manager, was going to sit down and ask them some questions, which would have been a little unusual but okay. Then another server stopped by and told the shoppers that there was a website address they could visit to fill out a survey and receive a discount on their next meal. The shoppers were left shaking their heads and asking each other, "What was that all about?"

The shoppers were not sure they had really been chosen at random: perhaps the server needed to "randomly" pick them because he was new, or because the server was awful and that was Olive Garden's way of comping part of the meal. Only Olive Garden can answer that. The shoppers would have preferred good service.

An increasing number of organizations are using technology to proactively gain customer feedback at the site of the transaction, and, in most cases, they choose to have their employees administer it. Unfortunately, employees and survey software don't mix well unless the employees have a sense of why feedback is so important.

Panera Bread launched a survey program similar to Olive Garden's. It offered $1.00 off a meal to customers who visited the web address listed on the receipt and filled out a survey. The survey site was quite attractive and easy to navigate. Much of the information needed to log onto the survey was on the receipt, which allowed for easy tracing of the transaction.

Offering an incentive is an effective way of enticing customers to visit a store's website and provide valuable feedback, but here's the catch: Having all the "hardware" in place does not ensure success. Kevin and Brooke are regular customers at Panera Bread, and only twice out of several dozen visits did Panera employees inform us about the offer. Initially, we thought this was because the survey was random or periodically offered, so we went back and checked other Panera Bread receipts and found the offer on all of them. The last time an employee presented the offer to us he said, "If you go to the website …" His voice began to trail off inaudibly as he started to turn his head to the side.

So here you have a well-orchestrated program that is at the mercy of the "software," which is to say, humans. The people who are gathering and analyzing the data can only assume that employees are clearly and effectively directing customers to the feedback tool. After all, one envisions a memo going out to all store managers reminding them to have their employees make customers aware of the $1.00 discount offer. The manager dutifully reminds employees of what they are to say to customers. The employee makes an effort to deliver. What's the problem?

Our professional experience is that most consumers are totally turned off by the half-hearted delivery of corporate-mandated scripts. Customers almost expect employees to follow their pitch with "I'm sorry, they told me I have to say that." Our belief is that no script at all is better than a poorly executed script. Half-hearted efforts make the whole organization look bad and discredit all the work that went into implementing the program.

In order to avoid poor delivery, could Panera have chosen to avoid employee involvement in hopes that customers would notice the offer on their receipt? Yes, but the reality is that customers don't have the time or the inclination to examine their receipts for interesting pieces of information. Companies need employees to proactively alert customers to programs that benefit the customer and the company.

The Panera Bread employee we interacted with failed to do even the minimum of what he was asked to do. There is a chance he didn't even know why he was doing it, only that he was told to, so he did. In his mind, he probably thought he should get points for remembering to make the offer. Think about it, what's in it for him? How is anyone going to know if he did it or didn't do it? What does he care if people get a buck off a sandwich?

As in all customer service systems, the most critical factor is what the manager does with the directive. If the directive is to be carried out successfully, execution of the program should include—but not be limited to—the following considerations:

- Employees should know why they are being asked to make an offer.

- Employees must realize they are being asked to sell the offer (with an explanation of what that means) as opposed to simply taking orders.
- Employees have seen the website survey, and they understand the intent and value of the research.
- The manager has observed each of the employees delivering the offer and coached them on how it can be done better.
- The manager has been authorized to establish a rewards system for the employees who have made the offer a specified percentage of the time.
- The organization or manager has solicited consumer observations on how the offer is being perceived.
- The manager has the right employees in place for executing the directive.

The last consideration of having the right employee in place is a fairly sensitive one, because it is difficult to find and keep service workers. However, managers must make a special effort to ensure that employees understand and can effectively deliver offers or be prepared to make personnel changes.

Keep the Customer

Being proactive does not have to be a spontaneous, creative act; it only needs to appear that way to customers. In fact, employees who in the past have been more reactive with customers can appear to be proactive if they can learn to anticipate customer needs. Therefore, what comes across as proactive is really preplanned. An effective method for learning to anticipate customer needs is for employees and their manager to role-play a wide variety of customer service situations.

Perception Strategies recently launched a customer service board game called *Keep the Customer*™ (www.keepthecustomer.net) to help employees practice many of the *turn ons* featured in this book. The game teaches employees to be proactive by allowing them to work through numerous customer service scenarios specific to their industry. A call center edition and a healthcare edition were the first to be created with more to follow. An online training version will also be developed.

Keep the Customer utilizes Customer Service Scenario cards, Role Playing cards, and Service Recovery cards to place employees in a variety of situations. A facilitator, with the support of a comprehensive Facilitator's Guide, determines if the employee's response is satisfactory, which allows them to put a token in the Loyal Customer circle or unsatisfactory, which causes a token to go in the Lost Customer circle.

Tools such as *Keep the Customer* are effective because they allow for a group of employees to interactively learn and grow. Together they can borrow from the best practices presented by fellow players and the facilitator while avoiding the pitfalls experienced and shared by other players. They also allow employees to benefit from scenarios that serve as trial runs rather than learning the hard way with real customers.

Tools

Explain What You Are Going to Do for Customers

Employees increase the customer's level of confidence by communicating the steps an employee intends to take to ensure the customer's satisfaction. Encourage employees to use phrases such as "Once we get off the phone, I am going to verify that your order is in process" to proactively diffuse any confusion the customer may be experiencing over what is going to happen next.

We recommend conducting departmental brainstorming sessions to identify the things most requested by customers and developing consistent responses.

We also recommend developing role-playing scenarios to simulate customers having to wait and what could be done to alleviate their discomfort:

- Explain to customers ahead of time why there will be a delay, letting customers know who will be assisting them and approximately how long it will be. Discuss with staff dialogue that is appropriate during a delay. What would they like to hear when they are forced to wait?
- Make up for a customer's inconvenience.
- Use recovery techniques such as how to handle customers unhappy with their wait.
- Have the person receiving the person-to-person "hand-off" introduce himself/herself and their position.
- Apologize for any wait regardless of the duration.

Offer Names and Numbers

Remove the burden of having customers look up information by providing it to them, such as names, telephone numbers, and website addresses. This act is often seen as initiative that exceeds the customer's expectations.

Ask Questions

The simple act of asking questions enables the employee to give more information tailored specifically to the customer's needs; imparting a confident, credible impression that gives the entire organization a feeling of credibility and competency. It has the further effect of making a customer feel cared for and valued. Conversely, when an employee does not bother to ask questions, the result is often a frustrating exchange that leaves many questions unanswered in the customer's mind.

Chapter 14
Helping Customers Make Decisions

> "These days, employees are making it harder and harder for us to spend our money."
>
> —Kevin and Brooke Billingsley

Key Levels needed to support the turn on:

3. Directly and Routinely Observe Employees in Action
5. Establish Accountability for Frontline Success

Every single day, we are all exposed to service providers who give us the impression they don't care if we give them our business or not. How can that be? Weren't they all hired with the singular mission of helping us? More accurately, to help us spend money? Why is it so hard for businesses today to connect the dots for employees? The message from management should be clear: "We pay you to get customers to spend money. The more they spend, the more secure we all are." One way to increase sales is to hire employees who possess the confidence to give customers honest advice, either solicited or unsolicited, and do it in a way customers appreciate.

"They don't let us eat the food."

Having worked in the restaurant business years ago and thus having a soft spot for servers, Brooke often poses a question about the menu out of deference to the server's advanced knowledge of the cuisine. At lunch one afternoon at a prestigious members-only club, she asked the veteran server, "What do you recommend?" We were surprised when the server responded matter-of-factly, "They don't let us eat the food."

This "high quality" restaurant violated an important rule of customer service. They completely broke the line between the seller and the product. They forgot the function of a server! Who should know more about the food in a restaurant than the consumer's direct connection to the kitchen? Some shortsighted mandates such as "thou shall not consume the food" handcuff employees and create barriers with customers. There should be no question within the context of a dining experience that cannot be answered by a server.

What Is the Difference between Selling and Customer Service?

Customer service and selling converge when employees understand that everyone is a customer or at least a potential customer. When consulting, we often ask executives to think about what percentage of the consumers their organization comes in contact with is actually made up of customers. If one considers a universe of contacts consisting of employees and their families, friends, vendors, donors, clergy, neighbors, and other businesses, then customers make up only a fraction of the potential customer base. We then ask them what their customer service strategy is for influencing this larger consumer base.

Organizations expect—or should we say *demand*—that their salespeople deliver, but often they do not demand the same of service people. Take, for example, a car dealership. We all know that the person who meets us in the lot is going to try to sell us a car and that his or her future with that organization is measured by his ability to sell. What about the employees who are "merely" providing a service such as the receptionist, the parts manager, or even the service manager? Are they held to the same standard regarding their customer service outcomes? Will they lose their jobs if their customer satisfaction numbers falter? If the organization demands customer service excellence they will!

Customers are turned on when every employee is held responsible for helping customers make decisions. Could a car dealership receptionist really contribute to a customer's decision to buy a car? We think so. For example, an acquaintance of ours drives a Lexus because she can't imagine having her car serviced anywhere else. At the dealership, the receptionist works in concert with the other employees to create an inviting environment. The point is that everyone must work toward the same goal of persuading customers to stay customers. And in this case, that is long after the salesman has sold the car.

As we go through our daily lives, we rarely feel we are being "sold to." And yet, that is exactly what we, as customers, want. We want to be sold on the fact that we are dealing with people who care who they hire, understand why the consumer matters, are knowledgeable about what they are selling, and believe in what they are selling.

Employee Identity Closes the Loop

Unless a customer encounter is recorded, as in a call center situation, the degree to which an employee is willing to help customers make decisions is an individual employee choice. Rarely will anyone know that an employee extended himself or herself unless the customer chooses to make a comment, and that is only possible if the customer knows who they talked to.

There is a tremendous amount of good faith in customer service because there is often no way for management to know what employees are doing every minute of the day. They must trust that employees will take advantage of opportunities to help customers make decisions.

Unfortunately, employees who refuse to identify themselves to customers believe that they can provide poor service and no one will be the wiser. A mystery shopping call to a retail store revealed how one employee secretly refused to take ownership.

"Hi," the shopper said, "I was just wondering... I saw this ad in the Sunday paper that said all DVDs are on sale. Is that true at your location?" "Yep," the employee said. "Okay, cool," the shopper responded, "How long are they on sale?" Again, a short answer, "'til Saturday."

The shopper wanted to see if he could throw the employee off a little, or at least make him answer with a longer sentence, so he asked if he could bring in the ad after Saturday and still get the sale price. Nothing doing, though. "Nope," was all the employee said.

Then, the call took a strange turn. The shopper thought he would ask the employee for his name and then be done with a successful, albeit brief, telephone call. So he asked for his name, explaining that the employee had been so helpful that he'd look for him when he came in to buy a DVD player. "No," the employee said. "What?" the shocked shopper said. The employee replied, "No. What do you need my name for? You don't need my name."

"Well," the shopper said, kind of thrown, "I thought you might get credit for a sale if I did it through you or mentioned your name." "I'm not here that much," the employee said, "I don't think you need to know my name." Then he hung up on the shopper.

This experience reinforces our firm's findings that employees who do not wear name badges (when they are required to do so) are more likely to produce dissatisfied customers. The same is also true of employees who do not give their name on the telephone.

As this example shows, some employees believe their anonymity gives them license to step outside the boundaries and be rude or unhelpful without customer retribution. Management must take steps to ensure employees identify themselves to customers, send the message to all their employees that lack of ownership is a serious offense that will be dealt with severely, and then follow up on that claim.

Customer Service Selling

Employees cannot sell or cross-sell products and services unless they are knowledgeable about what the organization offers. We like the term "selling" in relation to customer service because it implies a specific mindset. The difference between traditional selling and what we call "customer service selling" is usually determined by the employee's job description and how they are evaluated. For instance, in traditional selling the employee's income is tied to sales quotas or other tangible outcomes. These outcomes are monitored and tied to the organization's bottom line. Customer service selling suggests an environment where employees who have direct customer contact, but are not evaluated on sales figures, are individually evaluated on their ability to advance business through other forms of measurement, such as customer satisfaction and mystery shopping scores.

Perception Strategies regularly conducts mystery shopping studies to individually evaluate employees using customized scenarios such as an employee's aptitude for cross-selling, and imparting product and organizational knowledge. A minimum number of shops are performed for each employee based on his or her schedule so that strengths and weaknesses can be assessed. This information has provided client managers with a valuable and timely coaching tool.

In this increasingly aggressive selling environment, employees are trained and measured on their ability to direct business. They are responsible for expanding customer relationships with the intent of increasing the number of services sold or by referring customers to other areas of the organization.

Customer service selling means that an employee takes the time to explain the benefits of the department or organization in an effort to persuade the customer to use or reuse a particular service. The ultimate goal is to not risk customers going elsewhere because they've been forced to decide on their own.

Any service organization can achieve dramatic increases in business if employees are trained and encouraged to take advantage of selling opportunities. In order for increased sales to occur, three things must happen. Employees must understand the financial benefit to the organization and themselves, be able to recognize a sales opportunity, and know what services are available within the organization.

The magic in making the leap from a service organization to a service organization that *sells* is that with a subtle suggestion to a customer, new business is achieved with virtually no additional expense.

For instance, consider the value to a department store if the salespeople in apparel would make informed referrals to the shoe department or jewelry. Instead of simply selling a dress, what if they said, "You know, I have the perfect shoes in mind for this dress. Let me take you over there and show you. Then I'll introduce you to one of the salespeople who would be happy to assist you." However, this example does not come without some effort. For this to occur, the employee must keep abreast of the shoe inventory and also have a relationship with the salespeople in the shoe department.

Having every employee selling the organization is the ultimate win/win situation. It becomes easier for customers to maneuver through your system while the organization is incrementally generating more revenue.

There are many successful ways to disseminate information to consumers, yet none compare to the immediacy, efficiency, and flexibility of a well-informed workforce. Your employees are your best resource for quickly getting customers to the right department, and so on. Given this, your marketing efforts should be directed as much at your employees as your consumers.

The only thing that can nullify an effort to sell the organization is an employee's bad attitude. If customers don't like the way an employee says it, they won't hear what is being said. This is the criticism we have of scripting. Simply providing employees with the right things to say doesn't ensure customer satisfaction if the words aren't delivered with a genuine desire to help meet the customer's needs.

"All the doctors are good."

Mandates can sometimes serve as blanket protection to ensure that no one outshines anyone else or is given preferential treatment. In working with clients in the healthcare industry, our mystery shoppers will occasionally pose as a "new patient" and ask physician practice staff if they would recommend a physician. Frequently staff members will cheerily respond with, "All the doctors are good," thinking they have made a positive contribution to the practice and also avoided internal retribution from the doctors. Yet, consider the value to consumers in the "all the doctors are good" statement. These prospective new patients have been precluded from advancing one step closer in their decision-making process. The staff has managed to block the ultimate reason for customer service, which is to positively influence consumer decision-making.

Do patients respond favorably when a physician's office employee tells them a particular doctor is good? We think so! Customers want to know that they are stepping into an environment where the team members know and support one another. There is a great deal of inherent trust in healthcare, and most customers are not cynical enough to think someone would enthusiastically endorse a physician just to get them in the office.

Consumers know a smoke screen when they see one. They are smart enough to know that the person they are talking to has an opinion about the doctors in the office. We are not suggesting that they go against the wishes of the physicians and violate the policy of not making referrals. We often run into the unwritten rule in healthcare that employees refrain from giving personal preferences. But on those few occasions when an employee shares an opinion with our mystery shoppers, the customer's perception of that employee is overwhelmingly positive. That favorable impression is then transferred to the practice because the employee is their ambassador. If no recommendation is made, the consumer is no further ahead. They would not have asked in the first place if they did not truly want an answer.

Suppose when asked for a recommendation, the staff member responds with, "Because of your mother's age and her medical condition, I would recommend Dr. Jones. He is very kind and he is especially good with senior patients with the same illness." Instead of "they're all good," wouldn't a consumer rather hear a personal recommendation from a professional who works with the doctors and knows their abilities? If staff is unable to recommend a particular doctor, perhaps it says something about the doctor and how patients and staff perceive him.

While the majority of physician referrals come from family and friends, we contend that the best source imaginable would be office staff. Who is better qualified to know which physician would provide the best fit? Instead of insulting the consumer's intelligence with a statement that, even if true is unhelpful, the key is to train staff to ask questions that will help ascertain what the customer's preferences are.

Regardless of the industry, we recommend that you interview referees to better understand their preferences related to referrals. Both the referrer and referee can feel more comfortable as they work together to help customers make wise and informed choices.

Darla's Fireworks

It is nearing the 4th of July and, as usual, Brooke's uncle has waited until the last minute to go to the portable fireworks stand located in front of a neighborhood gas station. Every year he seems to get the same package of fireworks. He expects that these fireworks will work adequately, because they have in the past. If not, he can always go to the next stand down the road.

When he goes to buy fireworks this year, he notices that the person helping him is friendlier than usual and dressed better than he remembers. She even introduces herself, "Hi, my name is Darla." She helps him pick out the fireworks and takes a little extra time to give him advice on how to properly use them. She then talks to his children about safety issues. She relates a personal story to him and his children about a friend who was injured mishandling fireworks.

Brooke's uncle thanks Darla for her help, but before leaving, she tells him about some excellent fireworks that were new this year but that she doesn't carry yet. She gives him directions to a place where he can purchase them. She says these new fireworks will make the holiday even more fun.

Darla puts Brooke's uncle on a preferred customer mailing list that lets him know what they will be selling next year, when they will be setting up their stand, and how he can pre-order his fireworks online. Darla then gives him a business card as a reminder.

The 4th of July finally arrives. As he lights the fireworks, he is reminded of the safety advice the saleswoman gave him. He even recalls her name, Darla. The whole family is in awe as the fireworks—including the new ones Darla suggested—shoot into the sky one by one. Several neighbors ask him where he got them. He came to the conclusion that these were by far the best fireworks he has ever purchased, and he makes a note to e-mail Darla to thank her and ask her to add a few more names to her mailing list.

With very little effort, Darla provided a continuously high level of customer service that drastically differentiated her from what Brooke's uncle had come to expect. By personalizing the experience, she quickly laid the groundwork for a long-term relationship and was also able to plant the seeds for future business.

Tools

Educate Employees on Product Knowledge

Every organization must weigh the potential revenue generated by increasing employee product knowledge and the cost associated with the time it takes to help customers make decisions. Taking the department store example where the apparel department employee escorts the customer to the shoe department, the difference could be selling a $150 pair of shoes versus the customer going to the shoe store next door. The cost to the organization is the ten minutes it takes an employee to scan the shoe department to get acquainted with what is available.

Save Customers Time

Helping customers make decisions also saves them time, which is usually much appreciated. Employees should approach customers with a "one stop shopping" mentality. The more time you can save them by meeting their needs in your organization, the more they appreciate it. When employees use phrases like the following it gives customers the opportunity to think about how your organization can help them:

- "Have you thought about …?"
- "We also have …"
- "Is there anything else we can get for you?"

It is important for organizations to avoid using suggestive phrases as part of a script. Suggestive phrases must follow careful listening and be perceived as following a natural progression from the customer's original need.

Customer Service Selling

Customer service selling is a way for organizations to train and evaluate employees who are not evaluated by sales figures but have direct customer contact.

The components consist of:

- Training employees on product and organizational knowledge (who we are and what we do).
- Developing and maintaining interdepartmental relationships to encourage personal referrals.
- Individually evaluating employees on their ability to advance business through product and organizational knowledge, and cross-selling.
- Using other forms of measurement such as customer satisfaction survey and mystery shopping scores to assess employee effectiveness in directing business.

Recommend the Competition

Employees should always try to sell the organization. However, when a product or service is not offered by your organization, it is best to provide whatever information will help customers even if it means directing them to the competition. Customers remember and appreciate those who help them get what they need.

The Telephone Is a Sales Tool, Not a Necessary Evil

We recommend conducting a study to determine the nature of all calls to your organization. Recorded messages should be created to address the issues that could potentially lead to sales. For instance, if customers are looking for detailed information that does not require a live person, a message should direct customers to the organization's website.

Chapter 15
Taking the High Road

> "The customer is not always right, but they always know when you don't care about them."
>
> —Kevin and Brooke Billingsley

Key Levels needed to support the turn on:

1. Communicate a Never-Ending Commitment to Excellence
3. Directly and Routinely Observe Employees in Action
4. Utilize Coaching Techniques

It is a customer *turn on* when employees can take potentially confrontational situations and turn them into positive experiences. Taking the high road means never questioning, contradicting, or correcting customers. It also means the employees never verbalize the concessions they have made, such as "I'm not supposed to do this but . . ." Instead, employees use language that puts the focus completely on customers. Taking the high road not only implies that the customer is never wrong, but also that the organization is unified with one intent—making it right for the customer.

Jumbo Man on the Jumbo Jet

Being the last ones on a crowded United Airlines flight to Las Vegas, our family noticed that the further we moved toward the back of the plane, the more people stared at us. When we finally reached our assigned seats, we understood why. As the aisle cleared, we could see that someone in our party was going to be sitting next to a man who easily weighed in at 400 pounds. That someone was our youngest son, Jordan. Jordan, who was a cross country runner at the time, was about six feet tall and all of 125 pounds. As skinny as he was, his rear end was halfway in the aisle and his legs were sticking out at a 45-degree angle.

Brooke immediately brought the situation to the attention of one of the flight attendants. She pointed out that our son was unable to sit normally and that there was a rule that prohibited large people from taking up more than his or her allotted space. The flight attendant just stared at Brooke. She then said, "I'm sorry ma'am, this flight is full." It was fairly apparent that the flight attendant had no desire to address this uncomfortable situation.

Brooke decided to take a different tack and appealed to the flight attendant's focus on safety by reminding her that our son's safety was in jeopardy. "Okay," the flight attendant said. But instead of dealing with it herself, she headed up the aisle. About this time it was pretty clear to everyone in the back of the plane what was going on, including the very large man who was looking straight ahead quietly.

A few minutes later, the employee returned with the head flight attendant. Before any action was taken, Brooke became the recipient of some nasty glares as if to send the message that she brought all this on. The next move was totally unexpected. The head flight attendant said briskly to the large man—in a manner totally uncalled for—"Sir, will you follow me! We have a seat for you in first class." That's it. That's all he said. The situation had gone from bad to worse.

Perhaps we should have been happy that for the next four hours, our son was not going to be pressed against this massive man who could only get to his new seat by walking sideways. However, I did wonder in the name of great customer service why my son wasn't offered the first class seat. After all, who was inconvenienced the most?

You would think that this was the end, but it was apparently important for the original flight attendant to once again remind us of the dilemma *we* had caused. Just prior to landing, as Jordan slept peacefully with his headset on, the attendant rudely shook him awake so that she could retrieve the big man's baggage.

It wasn't just that these United flight attendants were prepared to violate their own rules regarding oversized passengers; it was that they were going to disregard the convenience and safety of another customer as they did it. I am certain that if the airline had been more conscious of this man's size and dealt with it at the ticket counter; they would have handled things more professionally.

The lesson we learned was "remind the airline of its rules at your own peril." The lesson for the airline should be to take the high road: treat everyone with respect and accept and fix the problem without assigning blame. Employees should be encouraged to embrace problems, and, when possible, they should be rewarded for solving them and be asked to share their solutions with the rest of the organization.

When Customers Get Nasty

The more space employees can give customers, the better chance of diffusing confrontational situations. The goal is to always avoid resistance. But often employees feel compelled to get into a tug of war with customers. Instead of tugging back, employees need to "give more rope" through patience and by being understanding without making excuses or blaming someone else. For instance, if someone complains about trying to get a live person on the telephone in another part of the organization, it is much better to simply say "I understand" than to say, "I know exactly what you're talking about. It happens to me all the time."

A Billing Department manager sought advice from us on the issue of customers cursing at her employees. Asking a caller not to use profanity is a form of resistance, but a necessary one. That is where tone of voice comes in. How it is said means everything. It has to be firm but non-threatening.

We recommended that she offer to have her employees express their desire to rectify the situation by saying "I want to help" or "How can

I make this right?" However, employees must avoid saying, "I want to help, but first you need to ..." Tradeoffs simply irritate people more. It has to be unconditional "love."

Employees should appreciate that the situation probably can't get any worse than it already is. That is, of course, unless the employee provokes or threatens the caller. Going toe to toe with a customer, so to speak, never works. Instead, the goal is to have employees feel good that they are sometimes able to turn the situation around.

Because there is no reason to take abusive calls personally, managers might want to turn it into a game by having staff share how many nasty calls they pulled out of the fire and then explain in detail how they did it. Being successful at handling these calls takes an understanding of the dynamics of confrontation and then practicing the art of recovery. With the proper approach, these situations really can get easier.

Explain to Diffuse, Not Light a Fuse

A hostess at a well-respected restaurant guided two shoppers past several available tables to seat them near an exit. We can appreciate the concept of sections and the need to distribute customers evenly among the wait staff, but the shoppers reported that this was not a good table. When they asked the hostess for another table because they didn't want to be near the exit, she explained that it was not actually an exit, but a door to the hallway. The shoppers felt like blurting, "How stupid of us, that makes all the difference!" They still wanted to move.

Service providers should never attempt to give an explanation if all they intend to do is show up the customer. Instead of achieving a point of mutual understanding, an employee's righteousness merely lights a fuse that leads to a slow burn for the customer.

Customers Like Being "Handled"

The idea of being handled may seem to have a negative connotation, but that is only if the one doing the handling is condescending or inept.

Handling someone requires a high degree of customer service mastery because it involves listening and understanding what is important to people. For the customer, it can feel like a warm blanket on a winter's night to know that someone cares enough to push the right buttons.

Kevin's first career path job was as a public information officer for the city in which he grew up. Through on-the-job training, he learned what it took to deal with an unhappy public. Kevin experienced taxpayer wrath on a daily basis. One of the first things one learns about handling angry customers is that you let them talk out their concerns. In this way effective handling becomes transparent to the customer.

We have all found ourselves in situations where we were more impressed with the handling abilities of an employee, while magically caring less about the outcome. "I had to pay sticker price for the car, but boy was the dealer nice!"

Service providers who truly know how to handle customers don't do it as a subversive tactic to manipulate customers; they do so to remove unnecessary obstacles. Their efforts can seem effortless because they already know what all the obstacles are and have already carefully mapped out solutions.

One way to do this is to ask employees to keep track of all the issues brought up by customers over the course of a week or a month (depending on the volume of interactions). Ask them to discuss what the best pro-customer way to address the issue would have been and role-play proper responses. Making the effort to analyze customer situations will make it much easier for employees to more instinctively handle customer concerns in the future.

Outside-In Perception Exercise

Part of taking the high road is an ongoing dedication to improving the quality of your customer service. There is tremendous value in seeing your organization from your customers' perspective. It allows you to identify and remove unnecessary roadblocks to higher revenue and customer loyalty. The difficulty is that, as an owner or manager, it is hard to objectively change your perspective because you are too close to it and because having someone else do it for you comes at a price.

However, in lieu of conducting interviews or focus groups, a better understanding of how customers perceive your organization can be achieved by answering for yourself the kinds of questions you might ask customers.

Take your time and honestly answer the following questions:

- Have we made it obvious how much we appreciate your business?
- Are we in any way making things harder for you instead of easier?
- Based on your experiences with us, do you get a sense of what is important to us?
- Would you consider us a leader in what we do?
- Is there anything about the appearance or location of our organization that turns you off?
- What could we do to get you to think of us first when you need the products or services that we offer?
- If we didn't offer you the best price and/or location, would you still want to do business with us?

Think about how you behave as a consumer. What turns you off—inconvenience, sloppy appearance, employee indifference, poor attitudes, slow service, filth, anti-customer company policies? Can you identify any of these in your organization? At what point would you say, "I will never go there again"? Is it always the big things, or does an accumulation of annoying trivial items push you over the edge?

Asking a customer these questions in survey form might not get a well-thought-out response. Obviously, customers do not give your business the same attention you do. However, the outcome could be devastating if the customer's perspective is not taken seriously. Don't confuse the customer's seemingly superficial behavior with a lack of resolve. It is precisely that point that requires a closer look on your part.

It is easy to be lulled into the dangerous habit of running your business from the inside out rather than the outside in. But keep in mind that it is critical for you to keep an ever-watchful eye on how your customers perceive you and avoid this pitfall.

Apologizing Is an Effective Neutralizer

While an apology for causing an inconvenience does not constitute full recovery to the customer, it is one way to take the high road and goes a long way toward neutralizing the customer's frustration. When one of our mystery shoppers asked an employee in Outpatient Diagnostics about stress testing, the employee deferred to a doctor for the explanation of what was involved. She followed that up with "Sorry I can't be of more help." The mystery shopper cited the employee for being "as helpful as she was able." Without the apology, the shopper may have considered the employee unhelpful or evasive.

An apology is a neutralizer. In its absence, the following example can occur: "At the beginning I was put off by her abruptly putting me on hold, and then just saying 'Hi' when she came back on, with no apology or explanation and no question to encourage me to talk, such as, 'What can I help you with?'" The two key phrases are "at the beginning" and "I was put off." The encounter began negatively and will continue that way until something is introduced to level out the experience such as humor, pertinent information, or a willingness to take the experience to an acceptable conclusion.

Tools

Deter Employee Finger-Pointing

Our firm's mystery shoppers have at times experienced isolated employee comments that, when looked at collectively, may signal a general lack of employee respect for the organization. For example, an employee handed a customer a form and stated that it was "something my boss made up," as if to suggest she was not totally behind it.

Employees will sometimes point a finger at the organization to divert attention away from themselves. This should not be tolerated. Customers don't want to work with employees who aren't prepared to take responsibility on behalf of the organization.

Inform staff that the actions of other employees are a reflection on the entire organization and that it is appropriate for them to apologize on behalf of the organization; for example, "I am very sorry that that was your experience before, please allow me to rectify it."

One of the best ways to discover how customers perceive the working environment is mystery shopping. This approach will very quietly uncover the source of the finger-pointing. Then it is up to management to provide employees with tools that will allow them to provide appropriate explanations on behalf of the organization.

Show Tolerance of Customers

Quite often, our mystery shoppers will give an employee a negative evaluation because of their tone of voice, lack of energy, or inflexibility in dealing with customers who in the employee's eyes seemingly "crossed the line." In order to take the high road, you must educate employees that lines must never be drawn with customers. They need to understand that confronting customers is *never* beneficial to the organization. They should also give customers the benefit of the doubt because, as most customers are strangers, they may have misinterpreted or misunderstood them.

Chapter 16
No Preconceived Notions

> "You are free to feel sorry for a customer, but you are not free to pass judgment."
>
> —Kevin and Brooke Billingsley

Key Levels needed to support the turn on:

1. Communicate a Never-Ending Commitment to Excellence
2. Hire People Who Want to Serve Others
3. Directly and Routinely Observe Employees in Action
4. Utilize Coaching Techniques
5. Establish Accountability for Frontline Success
6. Reward Those Who Excel in Customer Service

The manager of a small sandwich shop near our office once asked Kevin what he did for a living. Kevin explained that he is president of a customer service consultancy that specializes in mystery shopping. He smiled and said, "Really? How are we doing?" Choosing to respond more as a customer than a consultant, Kevin said, "Well, you're a little slow at times." The manager immediately got defensive. "We're not McDonalds," he said. "People need to understand the process." Kevin told him, "I'm sorry, but they don't. Customers don't care about your process. That's *your* problem. They just want things fast." Unfortunately, the frustrated manager left the business a couple of months later. The shop closed its doors a month after that.

The manager held the preconceived notion that customers should appreciate what he had to go through to produce lunch fare. It is true that the shop was unique. Located in a quaint turn-of-the-century railway station, the menu consisted of light café-style food and blended drinks. Very little of what they offered was prepared ahead of time. However, the manager missed the mark because he failed to look at it from the customer's perspective. Most customers are simply trying to make the best use of their lunch hour. Unique is great, even an advantage, if you can deliver your product in the same amount of time as the other restaurants. He couldn't, and probably never would due to limited preparation space and an antiquated ordering process.

Some businesses mistakenly believe that they can dictate service standards to the customer. Like the sandwich shop manager, they gloss over how and why people make decisions. These businesses fail to take seriously the fact that customers make decisions based on a perception of whether or not the business is delivering what the customer really wants. Only when we find ways to put ourselves in the shoes of those perceiving us can we begin to meet—and then exceed—customer expectations.

The Hospital Pillow

To solve some healthcare clients' needs, we send mystery shoppers into their hospital for an overnight stay. With the help of the hospital and a participating physician, we admitted a shopper into a Louisville hospital as a "self-pay" patient to avoid the insurance hassles. The undesired outcome of this (which is valuable for the client to know) is that a patient who is self-pay is perceived as someone unable to pay.

Early on in the stay, our shopper concluded that her thin, lifeless pillow was not going to cut it. She pushed the call button and a nurse responded. "Would it be possible for me to get another pillow?" she asked.

"Honey," said the nurse in a slow, Southern drawl, "it would be much quicker for you to have your husband buy you one at the dollar store."

Either the nurse was saying in a nice way that she would get the patient a pillow when hell freezes over, she was slamming her own organization because she knew there were no pillows to be had, or she was labeling the patient. The mystery shopper wasn't certain, but she perceived it as the latter because it was consistent with the care she had received up to that point. Employees must be reminded that it is not for them to pass judgment on customers.

Unfortunately, this was only the beginning of a 24-hour glimpse into the kind of service customers get when they are thought to be poor. Everyday service is often sub-par in this country, but for those who are labeled, it is much worse.

"Have you been with us before?"

Customers hold a treasure chest of information that can be unlocked in the simplest, most inoffensive way if employees are willing to just turn the key. Teaching employees to "read" customers gives them the tools to understand customers better, provide better service, and sell more of your products and services. Employees could rely on databases to identify loyal customers, but a quicker solution would be to simply ask the customer, "Have you been with us before?" This question provides opportunities for determining and exceeding customer expectations, feedback, and relationship building. Everyone from hotel clerks to hot dog vendors can use the customer's response to formulate a strategy based on previous usage.

This approach is used effectively by Smokey Bones Barbeque & Grill, a restaurant chain new to Indianapolis. As customers are walked to their table, the host asks them if they have been to the restaurant before. If not, he or she explains how the audio controls can be used to listen to the multitude of televisions throughout the restaurant, among other things. Smokey Bones understands that first-time customers should not be treated the same as a "regular" customer.

Service providers need to be flexible enough to treat the customers differently based on their responses. All customers are important, but not all customers are created equal. If a hotel customer responds to "Have you been with us before?" in the affirmative, then an opportunity presents itself to ask if everything was to their satisfaction to determine if they are previously satisfied or unsatisfied users. If the answer suggests that they are returning happy, then the opportunity to go the extra mile exists by asking the customer what can be done to improve this experience over the last.

If the customer responds with something like, "I wanted to stay at the Hilton, but they're full. I stayed here last time and didn't like the way I was treated," here is a wonderful opportunity for recovery. "Sir, I am sorry your stay with us was not a pleasant one. Might I ask what went wrong?" The customer's response will provide valuable feedback. Now relationship building can commence: "My name is David and I can assure you that I will personally see to it that you are taken care of. Here is my card, please call me if there is anything I can do to make your stay more pleasant. Your business is very important to us."

If the customer says, "This is my first time," it is time for the service provider to ensure that it is not the last. "I'm so glad you chose my stand for lunch. My name is Sam, what's yours?" The next order of business should be relationship building: "You know, it takes me two or three times, but I have a knack for remembering names and what you order. So give me a couple more times and then you'll be able to say 'the usual.'"

Asking, "Have you been with us before?" may be perceived as chitchat by some customers, but they will also perceive that relationships are important to the organization. Caring enough to find out more about the customer's relationship can only result in a win-win for the customer and the organization.

Honda Dealership

Having previously driven a Honda Prelude and a Honda Accord a combined 400,000 miles, we thought Honda first when we went to purchase a car for our boys to drive. As is true in major markets, we had several Honda dealerships to choose from and selected a new Penske-owned franchise closest to home. With the backdrop of a bright and spotless showroom, we were greeted by a tall, dark, and handsome young salesman. A typical customer's sensory perception would respond with "full speed ahead," especially if you're a female car buyer.

Brooke did in fact take the lead as the salesman took us through all the preliminary discussions such as what model car we were looking for. Even though Kevin was taking a secondary position to Brooke through this period, when it came time to talk money the salesman turned his focus and posture toward Kevin. Knowing his wife as he does, Kevin instantly concluded that this guy's good looks wouldn't help him this time. And what woman would appreciate the salesman automatically turning to the man to discuss the finances? The salesman's preconceived notion that Brooke, as a woman, didn't care about finances, wasn't competent to handle finances, or simply didn't have the authority in our family to make the purchase decision became an enormous barrier to making a sale.

When the salesman gave us the "best price" he could for the car, Brooke explained that she wanted to do some price comparisons at another Honda dealership. The salesman said we weren't likely to do any better and emphasized that the dealership really wanted to move cars because the big guy, Roger Penske, was in town for the Indianapolis 500. We knew that if this salesman had not misread Brooke's authority, we would have driven a car home in the next half hour. Instead, we drove to the other side of town to see if we could get some respect.

We did, and we got a better price. When we hinted that Brooke was calling the shots, the salesman at the second dealership spent a few minutes discussing female buying power. He "got it," and, thus, he got the sale.

Preconceived notions cause employees to go full speed ahead without reading the cues customers are leaving; such notions often cause your business substantial revenue. Role-playing is the most effective way to begin to develop the patience and listening skills necessary to flexibly handle any customer.

Room and Board

On a quick trip to Chicago over St. Patrick's Day, we entered a furniture store called Room and Board. We were in the process of refinishing our basement, so we weren't simply strolling through the store. Our antennas were high. We took in the entire three-story building, testing sofas and debating accessories. Not once in the hour that we were there were we approached by a salesperson—not even an obligatory nod of recognition.

We understand that people say "I'm just looking" all the time. We do it too. But which is the worse evil—not helping someone who wants help or trying to help someone who doesn't want it? The cash register is the deciding factor. If customers truly want help and they can't find you, you are forcing them to move on. I will remember your store when I am deciding where *not* to go next time.

Does the management of this store really want to adopt the "don't bother the customer" policy? This is a dangerous preconceived notion. Did they conduct focus groups that told them that that is the best approach? Customers expect that you are going to ask them if you can help them. Is it a nuisance? Perhaps, but the absence of it is very dangerous. The tradeoff is a minor pain that the customer is already expecting, for potentially great pain when they walk away as unhappy customers, or worse, disgruntled non-customers.

Tools

Reading Customers

Customers come to your organization in one of three ways. They are wide-eyed new customers, confident previously satisfied users, or impatient previously unsatisfied users.

Make sure your employees understand that these levels exist and work with them to devise their own style of determining what level the current customer is on. Then help them to develop the corresponding strategies for building new relationships (new customers), improving existing relationships (satisfied customers), or recovering damaged relationships (unsatisfied customers).

Help Employees Identify and Discard Preconceived Notions

A recent study of millionaires indicated that most are very unassuming and choose not to flaunt their wealth. It is also a fact that more women are entering the workforce than ever before. Preconceived notions that employees hold about wealth, race, age, gender, or anything else are likely to be wrong. To avoid this managers should:

- Educate employees on the loss of revenue to the organization when customers are dissatisfied because they perceive they are being labeled.
- Encourage employees to assume everyone is a potential customer.
- Provide examples of people who are not what they seem and ask employees to share their own examples.

Chapter 17
Empowered Employees

> "I expect that our associates will walk with a little more bounce in their step and understand that this company is behind them and has respect for them."
>
> —H. Lee Scott

Key Levels needed to support the turn on:

1. Communicate a Never-Ending Commitment to Excellence
5. Establish Accountability for Frontline Success

The amount of respect customers perceive from an organization is equal to the amount of respect the employees feel from their employer.

It is a *turn on* for customers when an organization allows its employees to make decisions without having to go to a higher source and when employees are not encumbered by barriers that have no meaning to customers.

However, the employee who "gets it" is often trapped in a catch-22 between organizational barriers and doing what he feels is right for the customer. If he goes the extra mile in favor of the customer but violates a company policy, he runs the risk of being reprimanded. On the other hand, if he adheres strictly to policies in the face of customer backlash, he will be the focus of negative customer perception. The customer will identify him by name when they complain about the inflexibility of the *employee*—not the company! The employee will then be reprimanded when the customer complaint surfaces and he is questioned about his actions.

A Bread Shop Misses an Opportunity

A woman carrying 15 loaves of bread walks up to the counter of a Panera Bread and explains that the loaves were burnt and that she can't use them. She explains that when she originally arrived to pick up the bread two days prior, she was encouraged by the salesperson to give them a try. She would have been in sooner, but she had been sick and lives almost an hour away. She had called ahead to explain the situation and to tell the store she was bringing back the loaves. She said they were supposed to be gifts. She then explains that she had already talked to someone on the phone who told her to bring the loaves back in.

The employee behind the counter responds indecisively. He then says he needs to find the person she had talked to. The woman turns to her husband and says rather meekly, "I knew I shouldn't have taken them." The customer supplied this employee with all the information he needed to handle the situation, but he was not empowered to do so. As a result, he appears uninterested in helping the customer.

After several minutes, the manager arrives on the scene. A discussion ensues as to what her options are. She could get gift certificates, replace the loaves with another type of bread, or come back tomorrow. The woman opts for the gift certificates. She is so ill that she has to be helped out of the store by her husband.

Does the store's manager ever think to ask employees why they fail to take care of situations themselves? Or has he not given them the authority to do anything without him? With such authority, the employee who sold the customer the bread initially would have been empowered to throw the bread away instead of selling it, and the employee who talked to the customer on the telephone would have been empowered to smooth the way for a more customer-friendly resolution.

Could the customer have supplied a better scenario for extraordinary service to occur? Getting it right makes the benefit to the company exponential. Getting it wrong means the exact opposite occurs. It is important to remember that the customer's intent was to voluntarily spread Panera's brand to 15 people in the form of a gift. What is it worth to Panera to keep the customer? Assuming that each loaf represents four family members plus the customer and her immediate family, we calculate that the potential gain/loss to the bread shop is at least 64 customers!

In an organization that is prepared to recover business and recognizes opportunities to deliver extraordinary service, the decision is easy. The customer couldn't have spelled out the situation any plainer. She was talked into receiving an inferior product, she was forced to drive a total of two hours while sick, she called ahead to make sure she could return the bread, she had to re-explain the situation to someone ill-prepared to assist her, and she ultimately didn't get what she originally wanted. She was a lost customer.

How many chances did the store have to recover this customer? The first is obvious: don't let the customer walk out of the store with an inferior loaf of bread. Poor quality has an enormous cost in recovery expenses. Because the baker made a poor choice in handing the 15 loaves of burnt bread to the customer, the options for recovery become more expensive.

Since the customer called ahead to explain the situation, arrangements should have been made for her to pick up fresh loaves. Or, the manager could have done a similar calculation to the one we did and realize that it was worth the expense to drive the two-hour round trip to deliver the bread to the customer. Imagine the customer telling the amazing story of the bread shop delivery to every recipient of the gift!

Staff could have been prompted to meet the customer's needs immediately instead of hunting around for the person who talked to the customer on the phone. A system should be set up where employees can access information on specific situations. Wouldn't it have been better if the first person she came in contact with was in a position to say, "Hi Mrs. Brown, I am familiar with the situation regarding the burnt bread, and we are going to have that delivered to you this afternoon—and for your trouble, we are going to give you a $25 gift certificate."

Recovery can be transformed into extraordinary service when you are listening to the customer and looking for opportunities to turn bad situations into successes.

One can only assume that all retail chains have training manuals for their people on customer service, or they at least have policies on how to deal with certain situations. Many of them empower their employees to recover business that otherwise is going to be lost. Why, oh why, didn't it happen here?

Quite simply, they were not prepared to do whatever it takes for the customer. On a macro level, they were not ready to execute actions that would mean more revenue for the company. On a micro level, poor listening skills resulted in a lack of empathy for this customer. This would indicate that they are incapable of addressing the individual customer's needs.

The organization's customer service culture, not policies or training, dictates that they "like" their customers. If they like their customers, they should look for ways to resolve their problems.

Applebee's

At an Applebee's Bar and Grill, we did a double take when we realized how unexpectedly friendly our waitress, Melissa, was. When Brooke explained that the pasta entrée was not what she expected, Melissa politely commiserated and returned quickly with something new.

When she returned to check on our meal, she apologized and explained that the pasta is usually very good and that she was very sorry that the experience was not perfect. Melissa didn't make excuses and she didn't blame others. She invited us back again by telling us that she knew it would be better next time and then handed my wife a coupon.

Empowered employees don't simply say "sorry" with their tails between their legs or get a manager to make the "big decisions." Empowered employees exude confidence, and that is a customer turn on!

That night, Melissa *was* Applebee's to us. It is true that our perception of the service almost always outweighs our lasting impression of the food.

It is not that this is an extraordinary customer service story, but that it was so simple. Our job as managers is to teach others to do this. It is great if Melissa was just being herself, but that doesn't matter. Melissa did what every service customer provider should do: she took it upon herself to provide the kind of excellent service that ensures customers come back.

Why Should Employees Care?

No amount of training or motivation will change how employees deliver service if they don't believe in the organization's mission. I am not referring to the mission statement that was painstakingly assembled to convince everyone of the organization's noble intentions. Rather, we use the term *mission* here in the context of the organization's journey.

Let's compare this journey to a rafting trip. One of the participants in the raft hears the leader say how important everyone is to the success of the trip as he steers the raft. She notices, however, that she is sitting in the middle of the craft with several others doing nothing, while a few people man the oars on the leader's instructions. She thinks, "If I am such a key part of this journey, give me an oar; give me something important to do." However, the leader fails to notice. Inevitably, the employee decides that as soon as the raft is close to shore, she is jumping out, rationalizing that she won't be missed.

Through their own behavior and deeds, employers must answer the employee's unspoken question, "Why should I care?" To simply say "That's the business we're in," or "That's why we pay you," or "That's what the customer wants," is not good enough. It is not that employees don't hear the logic, it is that the right button hasn't been pushed. They are not responding because they are convinced that leaders genuinely don't care about them.

Kevin recently went to a conference in Atlanta and, after checking in, popped into one of the hotel restaurants to sit at the mostly vacant bar. The bartender seemed pleasant enough, so he asked her, "What is your motivation for being nice to people?" She said, without hesitation, that she likes the way it makes her feel when she is able to make someone else's day more pleasant. She then turned to her manager who was seated at the other end of the bar and playfully sought affirmation, "I provide great service, don't I?"

The fact that she was willing to include the manager in the conversation suggested that there was trust and respect in that particular work environment. What is even more interesting is that despite her proclaimed self-motivation, she looked to her boss for validation.

It is true that some people don't need external motivation in order to provide exceptional customer service. You know them—they're often two or three clicks brighter than the rest of the light bulbs. They feed off the good feeling they bring to others and inherently "get it." They are the ones you want waiting on your table, checking you through at the grocery store, or selling you a car.

We once believed in an educational approach of showing employees the effect customer satisfaction has on the bottom line. After enthusiastically sharing the organization's values, a light would then go off in their heads, and they would be spurred on by a renewed sense of commitment. We have since abandoned that belief.

Hal Rosenbluth says in *The Customer Comes Second*, "People do not inherently put the customer first, and they certainly don't do it because their employer expects it. Only when people know what it feels like to be first in someone else's eyes can they sincerely share that feeling with others."

Great service comes from the heart. People need a reason to serve that somehow fulfills their lives. They buy into the program because they believe in the value of what the organization is offering. It is the thing that gets the small business owner up in the morning. He knows that his contribution to society is as great as—or greater than—those who have chosen to serve a corporation.

Tools

Build Trust in Your Employees

Empowerment is impossible without managerial trust. If employees go out on a limb, support them and encourage them to do it with confidence. If you disagree with how an empowerment situation was handled, discuss with the employee how it might have been resolved without discouraging his or her initiative.

Managers Need to Lead by Example

Managers are perceived as closely by customers as frontline employees. When managers provide the same poor service as the people underneath them, one begins to realize that things can only go downhill from there. Destroyed is the illusion that there is a level in the organization available to right the wrongs and be the voice of reason.

Chapter 18
Consistency

> "Our character is basically a composite of our habits. Because they are consistent, often unconscious patterns, they constantly, daily, express our character."
>
> —Stephen Covey

Key Levels needed to support the turn on:

1. Communicate a Never-Ending Commitment to Excellence
3. Directly and Routinely Observe Employees in Action
4. Utilize Coaching Techniques
5. Establish Accountability for Frontline Success

Many employees allow the accumulation of past customer experiences, job-related pressures, personal issues, and even the time of day dictate the quality of service they provide. However, customers do not care about any of these "realities" facing an employee. To be honest, as customers, we pretty much only care about ourselves.

If customer service excellence is delivered consistently, we will be turned on and gladly keep coming back.

Everyone has an "off" day now and then, but when employees are steadfastly inconsistent, it usually means that they work in a corporate culture where they get to decide for themselves to what degree they are motivated and when to provide exceptional customer service. Every time an inconsistent employee attempts to justify actions that ultimately lead to customer dissatisfaction, listen carefully. The employee is revealing the sentiments he or she has for customers when the manager is not around. Chances are these employees don't even know that they are exhibiting contempt for customers.

The Mythical Origins of Bad Service

Customer service started going bad in this country when a store owner, let's say it was Mr. Olsen from *Little House on the Prairie,* decided that instead of being in the store every waking hour protecting his investment and personally ensuring that his customers were happy, he would toss the keys to the clerk and say, "You know how things work here, I trust you'll keep the store running the way I do." And so he did. He packed Mrs. Olsen into the wagon and went on vacation for the very first time.

When Mr. Olsen returned from his trip, everything looked about the same. However, on closer inspection the place seemed to be a little less orderly than he liked it. He then went to the cash register and, despite less revenue than he expected, concluded that no one had ripped him off.

Not wanting to cause a fuss, none of the store regulars, including the Wilders, were willing to tell him that the clerk opened late most of the time and was giving away free candy. They also didn't tell him that some of the new folks in town came in just once, didn't seem to get a lot of attention, and never came back.

Mr. Olsen got things back in order quickly, and based on what he saw, he decided being away was not such a bad thing. Mrs. Olsen started making plans to go on another trip. Any revenue concerns Mr. Olsen may have had were outweighed by the relief of making someone else responsible for the day-to-day operation of the store.

Then one day, a couple of the previous one-time customers, seeing an opportunity to provide superior customer service to the Olsen's, decided to open the same kind of store across the street.

The Pizza Hut Story

Growing up in Michigan, Kevin was always surprised at the lack of traffic at the Pizza Huts in the area. Even the store across the street from the largest multiplex theater in town was rarely busy. When we moved to Fort Wayne, Indiana and discovered that Pizza Hut was the place to be on a Friday night, we were intrigued and a little baffled. We thought, what gives? This is a national chain with the same nationally advertised products as the Pizza Huts back in Michigan. Yet, the patrons are lining up outside the door of every Pizza Hut in Fort Wayne!

It is conceivable that pizza is more popular in Indiana than Michigan, but we doubt it. It turns out that the answer is consistent, reliable customer service. There was also a clear commitment to the customer. The reason people went to Pizza Hut in Fort Wayne is because, unlike most chains, it was a flawless experience inspired by the franchise owner, Richard Freeland, and maintained by career-minded managers.

The success of the Fort Wayne Pizza Huts demonstrates that it doesn't matter what the product or service is; if it fulfills a consumer want or need and there is a commitment from the top to deliver it at the highest level, and the product or service are repeated over and over again, the benefits to the company are virtually assured.

What Happens to Employees When the Focus Is Put on Customers?

In the past, when we needed a home improvement store in proximity to our home, Lowe's is where we went. Then one day it was announced that a Home Depot and a Menard's were being built within a couple of miles of Lowe's. Now that we had choices, we were anxious to see what the response would be from Lowe's.

We intentionally went to Lowe's soon after Home Depot opened to see if there was any effect. Keep in mind that this particular store was, in our estimation, devoid of a customer service culture, despite the posted signs that declared their devotion to customers.

Sadly, on this occasion, we saw absolutely no change. It was still the same indifference we had come to expect. We then said a little prayer for Lowe's hoping that they at least had some loyal contractors who would keep the store alive because they weren't giving the rest of the customers a reason to stay.

Several months after that experience, something miraculous happened! Instead of being invisible, we were greeted warmly by every employee we came in contact with. At the register, instead of complete silence, we received a smile and a sincere-sounding, "Please come again!" And we recognized this from an employee who had been surly the time before. Hallelujah! Was it a coincidence? Were we catching employees on a good day? Had bonus checks been handed out that morning? We didn't think so. We think it was a delayed *corporate* response to the competition.

On the one hand, we say, "Good for them." On the other hand, it is unfortunate that the store's management team was not empowered or intuitive enough to mount an initiative on their own when they heard competition was coming. Such lapses in management can be the death knell for a business. If store management was not the initiator, it is unlikely they will be the maintainer, either, when the program loses steam.

Bennigan's

Contrast the Lowe's experiences with the one we had at a local chain restaurant. We were between show times at the movie theater, so we decided to catch a quick dinner at Bennigan's. When we arrived we were very efficiently handled by "adults" who were quite engaging. After we were seated, we explained our situation to the waiter that we needed to get to a movie at a specific time. Instead of shying away from a commitment by using the line "I'll see what I can do," he said he would see to it—and he did. Everything about the experience was perfect.

We don't believe customer service occurrences like this are ever an accident or a case of stars aligning. Rather, it is a cultural phenomenon. We have a strong sense for when experiences are being controlled. Every single person working at Bennigan's that night knew what to do to provide customer service excellence. And while we cannot measure this Bennigan's against any other, we believe the management of that restaurant was responsible for communicating to the rest of the staff the kind of experience they were expected to deliver. Clearly, from the language, maturity, flexibility, and professionalism displayed, there was someone close by with his or her hands firmly on the wheel. That prompts customers to return because they are confident that they will receive a consistent experience. This is the genesis of customer loyalty.

"I have been after them for two months, and I am not giving up!"

It is one thing to set standards, and it is another to hold people to them. A client of ours was unhappy with her call center staff's failure to end the call by asking customers if there was anything else they could do for them. "I have been after them for two months," she said, "and I am not giving up!" At every opportunity she would remind them of what she expected and would use recordings of calls and mystery shopping to track her staff's adherence to that standard and others. Her efforts are both admirable and successful—this is the kind of managerial motivation it takes.

Who would ever know that her staff wasn't asking the caller if there was anything else they could do for them? Conceivably, no one; but she was thoroughly committed to having the very best call center in the country and knew that each of the standards were there for an important reason. They were related directly to the values the organization had established and, therefore, were not open to interpretation.

Most organizations don't sustain a relentless insistence on excellence over a long period of time. One of the more regrettable reasons is that managers are fearful of what employees will say or do if pressured to sustain customer service excellence. Since there are enough forest fires, including being short-staffed, they choose to ignore the "small" matter of unhappy customers! Another reason is the time and attention necessary to see sustainable results. Our clients who see the most transformative results are those who become obsessed with customer service and have made it a full time job.

Customers Do Not Acknowledge Internal Boundaries

Customer service consistency is based on the faith that other employees will not drop the ball when it is passed to them. One missing link in the chain can irrevocably damage the prospect of a relationship, regardless of the strength of the other links. In time, the customer's perception of the service delivered will most assuredly expose the lowest common denominator.

While it is always preferable for the delivery of customer service to result in a long-term relationship, the majority of customer service encounters are short stranger-to-stranger experiences. That is why consistency is so essential. The goal must be to do whatever is necessary to fortify all customer contact points with capable people so that there is never a fall-off. Without consistency, organizations cannot offer the total experience.

In the executive summary reports we prepare for clients, we always highlight and analyze customer service trends identified over the course of the study period. For example, a trend we discovered at one client's call center was that every time a customer was transferred out of the call center and to another department, the level of customer service and professionalism dropped off dramatically. It became obvious that the client needed to educate their other departments about the standards to which the call center operators were being held, train the staff on telephone etiquette, and then hold them to the same standards as the call center.

Unfortunately, we were asked to remove this trend from the report because it was considered out of the purview of the department we were studying. In this respect, our client made a classic error; they failed to realize that customers don't care about a company's management or political boundaries. If you do not have control over the entire path of contact the customer takes through your business, you have just done harm to your relationship with the *customer* and the customer's relationship to the organization.

Organizations must create a system for internally sharing information, whether in verbal or written form, that details how customers perceive various department and operational groups. If there are concerns that feedback will not be well-received through an informal approach such as an e-mail between managers, a formal system where information is sent to a centralized area will help to keep resentment low and awareness of customer feedback high.

The Publix Lesson

In Florida last year, a shopper entered a Publix grocery store and made a purchase. When he went to pay for his groceries, the most he got out of his young cashier was the amount he owed. Zero eye contact. When it came time to give him an obligatory "thank you," she handed him the change as she turned her head to talk to a fellow employee.

Many customers have a strong negative response to situations like these because they feel they're being devalued. Who does the customer fault for this unsatisfactory experience? Some will fault the individual employee, and some will fault the store, but clearly the Publix management is responsible because they trained, or failed to train, this employee.

Publix Customer Perception Score: –1

A week later, this shopper was in another Publix store, which was having a "Christmas in November" promotion. A smiling young lady passed out coupons at the front door while attentive managers dressed sharply in Publix suits hustled around making sure everything was perfect for customers. The cashier was extremely pleasant as she rang up his items. Even Santa Claus wished him a good night as he left the store. The shopper was pretty certain he had walked in on a unique occurrence, but was nonetheless impressed with the electric atmosphere he had stumbled upon.

Publix Customer Perception Score: +1

People pass on their customer dissatisfaction to others insidiously. Well-documented research suggests that people will retell roughly twice as many negative stories as positive ones. Consumers will do damage to a company's reputation that is commensurate with the crime. But it is also the case that consumers will tell more people if the perceived infraction is greater.

The shopper's next visit to Publix will be very important in determining whether he remains a customer, chalking up the initial negative experience to one misguided employee. The reality is that if the shopper's next experience is unsatisfactory, he will most likely generalize his opinion to the entire Publix chain. In the mind of the shopper, a pattern of inconsistent performance is developing. He will not isolate repeated negative experiences to a single store or individual, because, as a consumer, he doesn't have to be that discerning. Only when the majority of encounters are fantastic will the organization be perceived as consistent and start to earn his loyalty.

Every Customer Exchange Is a Separate One-Act Play

Brooke was in Chicago to give a presentation to a group of call center employees on the annual findings of our mystery shopping project. She told our client representative that the quality of the calls to a particular operator, Sarah, were consistently higher than the calls to the other operators. He said, "Well, that's interesting, because her station is near my office, and I can tell you she's not always that pleasant off the phone." All Brooke could say to that was, "Good for her."

Sarah knew that to be successful, she had to behave as if each call required a singular performance. She seemed to adhere to Bossidy and Charan's adage, "We don't think ourselves into a new way of acting; we act ourselves into a new way of thinking." Sarah approached her job as if she was acting in a play, and every time the curtain went up she was ready. This consistency made her stand out as a superior employee.

How do you train employees to show "concern" for customers or teach them to be "genuine"? This effort starts with the attributes employees must present with every encounter such as immediate acknowledgment, smiling, and offering to be of assistance. At Perception Strategies, we refer to standards that should occur with every encounter as Fundamental Customer Service Skills. The basic standards of customer service must be emphasized, perhaps over-emphasized, from the moment an employee applies for a job to the day they leave.

The basics must become engrained in an employee's everyday behavior before he or she feels comfortable applying his or her own personal style. Once the basics are mastered, employees are able to establish and maintain a consistently high level of energy for each customer that they refuse to fall below, and can easily add to, if necessary.

Consistency is the only way to build a base from which to exponentially increase business and to avoid downward spikes in satisfaction.

Tools

"Your service may be monitored …"

Dissatisfied customers say, "I will never go there again!" One could substitute the words "go there" with "eat there," or "fly with them," or "stay there," or "do business with them," and begin to see the bigger picture of a society looking for new opportunities to make a change.

If the service industry relies so much on consumer choice to keep business going, then it only makes sense that observing frontline encounters should receive much more attention. What if the phrase "Your call may be monitored for training purposes" applied to *all* customer service jobs? We hear this recorded message used all the time by call centers, but the concept seems to be missing when it comes to everyday service. Extensive training of frontline people does provide valuable information on products, services, and benefits, but only direct observation of employees will tell managers if they have a problem—and then allow them to direct their energy toward a solution.

Managers can begin to involve themselves in the customer encounter process by:

- Listening to employees while they are on the telephone.
- Observing customer/employee interactions.
- Taking immediate corrective action when employees violate standards.
- Setting an example by walking the walk and talking the talk.
- Admonishing employees who speak negatively of customers.
- Following up quickly on every customer complaint.
- Having a formal mechanism for following up on all customer feedback.

Chapter 19

Responsiveness

> "An interface is human if it is responsive to human needs and considerate of human frailities."
>
> —Jeff Raskin

Key Levels needed to support the turn on:

1. Communicate a Never-Ending Commitment to Excellence
2. Hire People Who Want to Serve Others
3. Directly and Routinely Observe Employees in Action

Regardless of our occupations, we are customers nearly every day of our adult lives. And yet, we wonder why more customers don't take a more aggressive stance with employees, for example, "C'mon, you have to know how this is making me feel?" in recognition of the fact that employees, too, are customers at some point.

Responsiveness is a *turn on* when employees jump at the chance to serve the customer. Whether they are responding to customers because they are fellow human beings, or because ultimately customers pay the employees' salaries, employees must find the motivation to maximize every encounter.

There is an undeniable gap between work life and consumer life that causes many customer service providers to be unresponsive to customers. And yet, what does a waitress expect when she goes out to eat? What does a flight attendant expect when he is a passenger? What does a nurse expect when she is a patient in the hospital? How understanding are these individuals of sub-par service when they are customers? The answer is not very!

A question that permeates through this book is why is the bond we all share as customers and employees so weak? We offer three explanations:

1. Employees really don't know what turns customers on. They can't make the transference from customer to customer service provider because they inherently don't understand what it takes to provide great service or they have been improperly trained;
2. They know what they like but can't apply it to their own job because they don't possess the skills; or
3. They actually know what turns customers on but choose not to use that knowledge because they simply don't care enough to make the effort.

How do managers assess where their own employees fall on this scale? And given that, what can they do about it? There are seven customer service-related questions we feel every manager should be able to answer to determine if their employees are in a position to provide excellent customer service. These questions are intended to keep managers focused on customer perception. We encourage organizations to use these seven questions as part of the evaluation for managers who have responsibility for frontline employees:

1. **Do you know what customers think of your employees' customer service?** This question assesses the manager's attention to employee/customer interactions. Are they taking the time to observe employee behavior? Are they utilizing tools such as mystery shopping or customer feedback to understand the customer's perspective?
2. **Are your employees aware of what turns customers on?** This question can only be answered if the manager already knows what customers want and has discussed it with the employees. However, how does the organization know if a manager shares his employees' ambivalent attitudes about customers?
3. **Do your employees deliver service that turns customers on?** This question implies that it is one thing to know what turns customers on and another to put it into practice.

What interactive training has been conducted to ensure that employees practice their customer service skills?
4. **How do you assess if your customers are turned on?** This question forces managers to evaluate the tools being used and to discover creative ways to gain and use customer feedback. Is the organization ignoring or oblivious to signals of customer discontentment?
5. **How do you encourage consistently great service?** This question addresses the tools managers use to turn observation into action. Are managers prepared to be coaches to employees? Can they successfully get the most out of them?
6. **How do you get employees to care about customers if they are not happy in their job or they don't seem to like serving people?** This question speaks to the manager's ability to show leadership in support of the organization's values. Can the manager turn a marginal hire into a great one?
7. **What are you willing to do if great customer service is not provided?** This question is intended to determine if the manager is truly in charge of the customer service environment. Are they able to discipline or terminate employees for behavior toward customers that is detrimental to the organization?

Begin to challenge your employees by uncovering the customer service attributes that are important to them so that they can start to put them into practice for their customers.

In Search of Swatches

Brooke called a store that sells furniture by catalog to take advantage of their 20% off sale on upholstered furniture. She needed to see a swatch first and was told that it would take up to two weeks to receive the swatches she requested. Brooke explained that she would miss the sale, to which the customer service representative (CSR) responded by asking her to hold as she checked on possible solutions with a supervisor. She returned without a solution. She apologized but said that they would not expedite the swatches sooner for her. Brooke explained that with all the competition in the furniture business, she had many other choices and would take her business someplace else.

That place happened to be a new William Sonoma Home store in Indianapolis. A catalog had arrived in the mail a few weeks after the store opening, prompting Brooke to call the catalog to request fabric samples. The customer service representative was very pleasant and professional, explained that there was no charge on the samples, and asked if there was anything else she could do to help Brooke.

Brooke felt taken care of and her first impression was that anything she ordered from this company would be handled professionally. The samples arrived at the time the CSR promised, and the service was matched by the quality of the items they sell in their stores.

Brooke's parting comment to the first company was not an idle threat, and they should have known that. We must all be aware that our competitors will gladly fill in and do what we are unable or unwilling to do. That's business. But the difference between Brooke and most customers is that she was nice enough to tell them she is going elsewhere. Statistics have shown that less than five percent of customers are willing to do that, which means that most businesses have no early-warning system in place to determine when they are losing valuable customers to a competitor.

The way the first company approached Brooke reminds us of the old Burger King slogan, except in this case "special orders do upset us." Organizations that are unable to respond to their customers will always be forced to look over their shoulders wondering when someone will swoop in and steal their business.

Greetings for Everyone

A few years back, Kevin attended a conference at the Downtown Marriott in Kansas City. Walking across the crosswalk between the hotel and the old Muelbach Hotel, he came to the conclusion that every employee should be required to smile and say hello to every customer they encounter. It bothered him that he couldn't get eye contact from the employees he walked past. But then, to his surprise, he got a hello from an employee who was dressed in a uniform and appeared to be a management type. As customers, we have the luxury of evaluating our experiences on any level we like, regardless of pay grade. So why is a greeting considered the right thing for a manager to do and not right for other employees? Aren't they *all* supposed to be glad to see customers?

If you wanted everyone to get on board with mandatory greeting initiative, how would you ensure that it was carried out? The first challenge is for the organization to communicate to everyone that the current practice of not smiling, not saying hello, and not giving eye contact is unacceptable. They can do this globally via whatever communications they have in place, or they can choose to pass it down through the management ranks. This is a challenge because it is highly unlikely that everyone is going to receive and retain the message, especially in an organization as large as Marriott. But for the sake of demonstration, let's assume that 100 percent of the employees have received and understood the message and were told why this new initiative is so important.

The second challenge is employee perception of the initiative. High performers will jump in and begin following the mandate immediately. Mid-level performers will wait to see what the high performers are doing and then cautiously proceed with an eye on the naysayers. The low performers will publicly give the initiative tacit approval, but privately trash the idea.

They will begin to ask themselves, "What will happen if I don't do it?" Then they will play out the scenario in their heads, "A customer walks by and I don't say anything, how will anyone ever know?" The low performer will then take it a step further and have a ready-made list of explanations for why they didn't give recognition to the customer, such as "The customer wasn't looking at me," or "I was actually off duty," or "I had already acknowledged them before," and so on. Of course these are all poor excuses and can be easily refuted. If low performers would realize that less effort goes into providing great service than the amount of energy they put into sabotaging it, managers and customers alike would all lead happier lives.

How managers respond to the initiative will depend on their own value system. There are also high-, mid-level, and low-performing managers. They will all ask themselves, "How do I fit into this?" High-performing managers will find a way to embrace the initiative, because the situation bothers them and they had already thought about instructing their employees to smile and say hello to all customers.

Managers with a mid-level of performance may question how important they think the initiative is, especially in light of anticipated employee backlash. However, they may also wonder if they can risk having a customer or mystery shopper complain about an employee.

Finally, like the low-performing employee, the low-performing manager lines up excuses for why the employees aren't following the mandate. It won't be a question of how to get the job done; it will be how to squeeze the life out of it so that customer service culture is forever at the mercy of the low performer.

Too much time and energy is wasted trying to bring low performers around. If an organization is serious about launching a culture-changing initiative, the more swiftly low performers are dealt with, the more opportunities there are to focus energy on managers who truly want to make a difference.

Kinkos

When consulting with clients, we identify strategies that frontline managers can use to become an active and positive force for change in their organizations. This sometimes involves managers having more direct access to customers. The resulting level of responsiveness can be a great turn on for customers.

Walking into the Kinkos we frequent most often, Kevin instantly noticed a change. He got the sense that it was somehow more efficient. Employees were extremely busy but abnormally nose-to-the-grindstone quiet. A middle-aged gentleman walked up to Kevin and asked if he needed help. Kevin told him that he was there for some binding. The employee quickly grabbed someone to do the binding job so Kevin didn't have to wait.

This employee had the persona of a manager or perhaps a corporate representative, as he seemed to effortlessly direct the action. What separated him from most managers was that he also served as the official greeter.

There was a refreshing sense that someone was truly in charge and orchestrating things. The employees were constantly getting someone else to do tasks that were easier or more appropriate for the other employee. There was little time for chitchat among the employees.

The whole time Kevin was there, he was *turned on* by the kind of behavior and efficiency that is possible when a manager is actively involved in day-to-day operations. Take the time to consider how much more efficient your operation would be if you were more active in directing customer flow. Managers who are this actively involved set an excellent example for their employees and are perfectly situated to observe employee-customer interaction.

"Give Us a Call"—Take 1

What are customers to think when a business forces them to initiate all of the communication? One's first response might be to think that the company is making so much money they really don't care what the customer does. At least that was the sense a shopper got when she called a local collision shop to check on the progress of her car. This particular body shop was cranking out so many cars it seriously made her think about a career change. However, they crossed the line when the clerk said, "Give us a call to see when your car is ready." Even though her clerk agreed when the shopper soberly reminded Kevin of whose responsibility that was, the lesson is that organizations should never be too busy to serve the customer.

Like a new "hot" restaurant or store, the allure of "you're swamped, therefore you must be good" is only tolerated by consumers for a short time. Customers will eventually gravitate to excellent service, making some other body shop the hottest thing in town.

"Give Us a Call"—Take 2

Brooke went to Home Depot to buy new carpeting. She selected a sample and approached the salesperson. He said that he was leaving for the day and couldn't help her; however, he did give Brooke the name of the next person who was scheduled to come in. Needless to say, his unwillingness to stick with the customer did not thrill her! When an employee's shift is over and he needs to leave promptly, he should first introduce the customer to the employee on the next shift, and make the new employee aware of the customer's situation and needs.

When the new salesperson arrived, he said that the carpet sample Brooke wanted to take home needed to be ordered. "Call us in a few days to see if it is in," he said. He didn't say, "I'll call you." He didn't even say, "Call *me*." So as the customer, Brooke immediately had a vision of 5 or 6 more calls to get one carpet sample!

The extra effort to write down a name and give the customer a call was obviously not worth the potential sale. Nor was staying with the customer long enough to determine that the sample needed to be ordered, thus saving the customer the time of waiting for another employee to arrive.

Is that really the kind of responsiveness the brass at Home Depot intended? We seriously doubt it. Predicting the willingness of your employees to do whatever it takes to make the sale is difficult to measure. And yet, if you are in tune with how your employees respond to and value customers, you can begin to predict which employees will go the extra mile when you are not there.

Pizza Nazi

We decided to drive from Indianapolis to New York City for a spring break of sightseeing and Broadway. With two teenaged boys in tow, we entered the city tired and hungry from the daylong drive. We hit the streets looking for something in the fast food category. At approximately 9:00 p.m., we walked into a Sbarro on Times Square.

"Can I get a slice of pepperoni pizza?" asked our son.

"No more pepperoni, closing soon. Come back tomorrow," the pizza maker said with a straight face and broken English.

Thinking this was a guy doing a Soup Nazi imitation and playfully indoctrinating us to the Big Apple, I laughed, "Ho, ho, you're kidding, right?"

"No pepperoni—what do you want?"

When we arrived at the table with cheese pizza on our plates, Brooke asked, "Where's the pepperoni?" We explained that, much to our surprise, *he wasn't kidding*. Kevin sauntered over to the manager and asked how late they were open. "Midnight," he said. Kevin explained that the Pizza Nazi was refusing to throw a pepperoni pizza into the oven. The manager showed an appropriate amount of credulity by saying, "He's got an attitude. I'll have a talk with him," but he was unable to recover from the damage that was done as we left with no pepperoni in our stomachs.

You can sort of excuse an experience like this because it is vacation, you'll be laughing about it for the next 20 years, and it was NYC. But the kind of service we receive every day at the businesses we patronize week after week is not so funny. Vacations are one thing, but quite frankly, bad customer service is affecting our daily way of life.

We may have other choices for the services we seek—groceries, gas, dry cleaning—but they are virtually all at the same service level. We would be inclined to say, "Hey America, get used to it," if it were not for the plethora of anecdotes that come up in regular conversations that suggest most people are not ready to accept unresponsive customer service. How often do you hear anecdotes such as, "It's a shame that business went under, their customer service was outstanding!" Not very often. Organizations that provide excellent customer service deserve to succeed and usually do.

What If Every Job Depended on Tips?

The purest gauge of responsiveness for customer service is direct compensation by the customer for service provided. What if everyone who provided customer service relied on tips for their income? True, some people are lousy tippers, but—at least in theory—gratuities are a reflection of how well you think someone served.

On a trip to San Francisco, we were studying a kiosk outside our hotel, trying to make sense of the trolley system. We were slightly unnerved by the sheer number of street people nearby yelling at us for no reason. We were afraid that making a mistake might end badly, so we were being very careful.

After a few minutes of standing there indecisively, a gentleman who appeared homeless walked up to us and offered to give us directions. He explained that there were a lot of people who couldn't be trusted, but he knew the system well. Our new guide helped us find the right trolley and also instructed us on how to get back. When he finished, he said in a soft tone, "I hope I've helped you; and by the way, I am not an employee of the city. Tips are appreciated." We were more than happy to oblige, not because he was homeless and we felt sorry for him (okay, maybe a little), but because he provided a much needed service.

You can probably see where we are going with this. If employees' income was left solely to the discretion of customers, wouldn't that change the way many of them behave? Wouldn't employees attempt to figure out on their own—without extensive training—what it takes to earn a bigger gratuity? The cashier at the grocery store might perk up, the flight attendant might go out of her way more often, and the clothing store employee might be more personable.

A tip-only system of employee compensation is obviously not realistic and would be a great burden on customers who, even on a short shopping trip, would be constantly doling out money to store employees. For the most part, customer service is a good-faith system. If good service doesn't occur, the customer's recourse is not to withhold money, but to leave and not come back. Therefore, it is important to try to get employees to make the connection between the customer service they deliver and what that might be worth to customers.

Using the "tips" concept, coach your employees by asking them to picture an environment where they are paid strictly on their efforts as perceived by the customer. Ask them, "Do you think you would do well financially in this environment?" You might also ask, "Do you believe customers are getting their money's worth?"

Responsiveness Is *Always* about People

A congenial, male postal worker in his forties was working behind the counter at a busy downtown post office facility. Moving rapidly through his line, Kevin stepped into place in front of him. He chuckled saying, "Didn't think we could work this fast, did you?" His demeanor, especially being a "dreaded" postal worker, was totally unexpected and delightful.

Another surprise encounter occurred in New York City. Recognizing that our flustered family was lost, a friendly New York City subway cashier came out from behind her booth to show us where we were on the map and what it was going to take to get to Battery Park and the Statue of Liberty. Her response to our obvious confusion was both unexpected and powerful; small, almost imperceptible events like that have a way of positively changing a visitor's perception of the entire city.

The responsiveness of these employees was memorable because they went contrary to previous experiences and the perception of the organizations they represent. Notice that the preceding stories were about people. "Extra mile" stories almost always are. One is more likely to share a story about a wonderful employee than the organization's efforts to streamline a process.

From an organizational standpoint, the goal of exceptional service is about the collective perception of the organization. Think of it as consumers keeping a quantitative mental scorecard based on the qualitative behaviors of your employees. When consumers are deciding where to take their business, they always consult their mental scorecard first.

The following statements from our mystery shoppers exemplify the power that employee responsiveness can have on the perception of the organization:

- "Brett boosted my opinion of this place immediately."
- "Overall, Melissa had a wonderful attitude and left me with the impression that the people in this department are friendly and helpful."
- "I wish my sister really was moving to the area because I liked Pat so much, I would love to send in some reinforcements for her!"
- "I wish I could rate Sheila higher than five [on a five point scale] because she was so nice and helpful, and I felt so good after talking with her. Seriously, if I did have a friend with cancer, I would definitely want them to be in her department."
- "This visit actually made me want to consider becoming a member because of how helpful and friendly Janis was."
- "I felt like we had a new friend in Stephen, and left with a very positive feeling about the organization."

These statements seem quite simplistic on the surface. And yet, they clearly show the powerful impact one employee can have on future customer relationships with the organization. They all seem to be saying, "I like what I got, and I want more!"

We urge you to utilize the comments you receive to illustrate for employees how in the eyes of the customer, one employee can positively represent an entire organization.

Tools

Pay Closer Attention to Customers When Not Busy

At times, employees are less busy than usual. Understandably, they congregate during these slow periods. It is important they not get so caught up in their conversations that they ignore customers.

Managers Must Walk the Talk

Customers expect that when they either request a manager or find themselves in the presence of one, they will get more empathy because the manager, by virtue of their experience and position, "gets it."

Treat Each Customer as an Opportunity

Keep it fresh. Act as if this is the first time the customer you are encountering has ever experienced your organization.

Chapter 20
Delivering on Promises

> "Promises are the uniquely human way of ordering the future, making it predictable and reliable to the extent that this is humanly possible."
>
> —Hannah Arendt

Key Levels needed to support the turn on:

1. Communicate a Never-Ending Commitment to Excellence
2. Hire People Who Want to Serve Others
3. Directly and Routinely Observe Employees in Action

There are two types of promises made in the name of customer service. The first is the promise an employee makes directly to a customer, such as "I will call you back as soon as your order arrives," "I will be right with you," "it will be 10 minutes," or "your shipment will be there on Wednesday."

The second type of promise takes place on a much larger playing field. It involves an organization's declaration that they are in some way committed to their customers, with the implication that they are *more* committed than the competition.

When a corporation such as Merck tells us they are "seeing things through the customers' eyes" or Citi credit cards asks us to "Dial 0 to get a live person," they are attempting to differentiate themselves from other companies who apparently see the world through greedy corporate eyes or never allow you to talk to a real person. These slogans promise a more respectful customer service experience or a more advantageous way for customers to do business. Companies that make claims of superior customer service do so because either they can back it up with service that resembles the claim, or they are telling consumers what they think they want to hear.

It is one thing for an employee to not follow through on a promise to a customer, but the stakes are considerably higher when a broad claim of superior customer service is made publicly. A promise not kept on this level is a "one step forward, three steps back" proposition. It is impressive that an organization displays the confidence to make a customer service claim and it may lure the customer in, but it can be disastrous if the customer perceives this to be a false claim. This most often happens when the company simply doesn't have the infrastructure in place to support the claims of excellent customer service.

We can apply Ken Hultman's definition of values in *Making Change Irresistible* to the issue of customer service claims: "A *genuine value* is one that actually guides a person's behavior, while a *bogus value* is one that the person claims to hold but doesn't act on." For instance, if Citi credit cards really does allow customers to dial 0 to reach a live person, then Citi is displaying a genuine value. If dialing 0 doesn't always work, though, some customers will conclude Citi has bogus values.

Hultman goes on to say that, "Bogus values often are easy to spot—discrepancies between what people say and do shine like beacons—but they're hard to change, because they become deeply rooted in the corporate culture."

Therefore, making claims of superior service not only has implications for how customers respond, but for how all employees are trained and managed. It presupposes that the existing workforce and all future hires understand how to deliver on the claim. The claim must also become so deeply entrenched in the culture that delivering it is second nature.

Promises should always be tested before making them public. Ensure that your organization can deliver by:

- Testing the promise or claim to current customers by conducting focus groups or intercepts.
- Going straight to the front line and testing it with employees to make sure they can sell it.
- Communicating the claim to all employees to get their buy-in.

"Magical Mission Statement"

We frequently went to the movies at a 16-screen United Artists Theaters' multiplex before it became a Regal Theater. Prior to the previews, we were starting to notice a United Artists slide under the heading "We guarantee a magical experience!" It went on to say, "If we have not exceeded your customer service expectations, please see the manager." We pity the poor manager who tries to enforce this promise! We immediately had a vision that if we played our cards right, we may never pay for a movie again.

What a nice, well-intentioned, albeit misguided, message. United Artists wanted us to believe that their employees, who are mostly teenagers too young to have significant customer service experience, were going to deliver on the promise of a magical experience. The truth is that working at one of these large multiplexes is too often one of those thankless, high-turnover service jobs where speed is king. Maybe United Artists was counting on the fact that customers wouldn't take the offer seriously because they are more concerned with how good the movie is rather than how the great customer service is.

Even though it was just one slide and not something plastered on every popcorn bag or soft drink cup, United Artists obviously thought customer service was important enough that they offered up the manager's time to make the experience right for customers. What would it really take for a business like United Artists to pull off this "magical experience"?

The answer is, create an environment that is noticeably better than the competition. Whether one takes a narrow view of the competition (video rentals and other theaters), or a broader view (any entertainment that costs approximately $40 for two people), the choices are numerous. When one Googles our zip code, at least six theater choices pop up within a ten-mile radius. Realizing what the theater is up against, it is surprising more theaters don't implement a customer service strategy.

Would more customers go to this theater if their customer service was better than anyone else's? We think so. What would it take? Eye contact, lots of smiling, a sincere greeting such as "Hi, welcome to Regal

Cinema" and a close such as "enjoy the show" would probably exceed most customers' expectations. For other businesses, however, these "basics" are only the foundation on which more sophisticated customer service techniques must be built. However, here's the kicker for the theater: those basics have to be delivered to everyone, every time. After about the fourth time at the theater, customers will reach the *turned on* point and think to themselves, "Something's different here. This is by far the nicest group of theater employees I have ever seen!"

There is one last roadblock, however. Will a better trained, more consistent group of customer service providers result in less employee turnover? We doubt it. It is still a low-paying job and the increased demands put on employees will likely turn some employees off. To achieve customer service excellence in this setting, the key will be to hire the right people (realizing that standards can't be set too high) and to develop a solid orientation program that sets the expectation bar high.

When you make a promise, you must remind employees daily that the bar created by the promise exists. If it's guaranteeing a magical experience for customers, it is necessary to continuously remind employees that they are there to make the promise a reality.

"Please Don't Hug the Cashiers"

Aldi's is a lower-priced alternative to other grocery stores. Their brands are less recognizable, credit cards are not accepted, shelves aren't stocked in the normal fashion, and speed through the checkout line is preferred.

Almost simultaneous to building a new store in our area, Aldi's launched a billboard campaign. It read, "Please Don't Hug the Cashiers." Brooke had to admit she was instantly impressed and amused by the slogan and intrigued with the implied claim of customer satisfaction. She decided to test this one out herself.

Based on her one experience, she thought the store was true to the intent of the billboard campaign, which is to suggest that Aldi's provides better service than one would expect. Not that Brooke wanted to hug anyone, or that she thought the service was exceptional, but her expectations weren't that high to begin with given the store's niche. The billboard caught her attention, got her in the door, and the customer service didn't disappoint her. As a result, the implied promise of the billboard campaign turned out to be as clever and beneficial as it intended.

If an organization makes a customer service claim, and every aspect of every experience reflects that claim, the value to the organization is exponential. This is due to the expanded audience made possible by marketing the promise and because the actual experience penetrates through the cynicism brought on by a glut of other companies' overreaching promises. Instead of ignoring the claim, this powerful *turn on* for customers is simply, "Wow, they really mean what they say!"

"Treat People Better"

A television commercial presently running in the Indianapolis market caught Kevin's eye. The commercial shows a man getting on an elevator with other passengers. He clearly has a more confident demeanor than the others, and when a would-be passenger races to catch the elevator, he is the only one willing to step forward and stop the doors so that the frantic passenger can get on. The narrator then says, "You can always spot our people." This is followed by an intriguing tag line on the screen which reads, "Treat People Better."

This commercial is for Hendricks Regional Health, a healthcare provider serving the communities just west of Indianapolis. Being so close to home, Kevin decided to test the "premise of the promise" in addition to sitting down with a hospital representative to understand how they intended to deliver on the promise.

First, Kevin wanted to know if it would be readily apparent that this was an advertising claim without teeth, or if he would experience an organization living out their bold challenge. From a few brief encounters with staff, it was obvious that the latter was true. There was no hesitation as a front desk employee (intentionally manned by a paid staff person rather than a volunteer) escorted Kevin to the meeting room. Every employee that walked by us verbally acknowledged us in some fashion. While this may not seem like a big thing, our experience as mystery shoppers tells us that a great deal about an organization's culture can be determined by an employee's willingness to greet a passerby.

Hendricks Regional seeks to maximize the Treat People Better campaign with a comprehensive approach that includes employees and the community-at-large in their mission. An example was the creation of the Treat People Better Opportunities program to encourage employees to participate in numerous community activities such as clothing and toy drives. They also started the Treat People Better Awards to highlight individual, business, and employee contributions to the community. The awards program featured finalists who "have gone above and beyond to treat other people with kindness, dignity and respect."

The message hidden behind the campaign is perhaps the single most important factor that allows organizations to deliver on promises: That is the complete support and conviction of the person at the top. The fact that Hendricks Regional Health CEO Dennis Dawes was an active participant in the program and a longtime leader in the community energized the campaign into a sincere force for change.

The lesson here is that it is not possible to challenge the community, let alone a television market the size of Indianapolis, and sustain an initiative of this magnitude without the full involvement and support of the organization's leader.

"Customer Service" Desk

On one occasion, Kevin was unable to get through to Customer Service at Best Buy and eventually hung up in exasperation. Thinking that with the assistance of another employee he could somehow circumvent the system, he pushed a number on the telephone tree that would put him in touch with the appliance department. The call was picked up by Ted. Kevin explained to Ted that he wanted to speak to someone in Customer Service but that no one was answering the line. Ted said he could transfer Kevin to Customer Service but added, "Don't blame me if they don't pick up."

Kevin asked him if he could find out why they weren't answering and Ted said, "I can't just run over there and make them pick it up, it's too far away." Kevin repeated his desire to talk to someone in Customer Service, and Ted immediately transferred him. After four minutes, Kevin hung up and decided that he wasn't going to get through. The entire experience lasted 16 minutes.

It may seem obvious but it deserves emphasis: the Customer Service Desk's only mission is to help customers. Any organization with a Customer Service Desk is making a commitment to customers that anything out of the ordinary course of business can be handled there. It is an implied promise.

The challenge is for the organization to live up to words *customer service* and to be the one place customers can be assured of getting customer-focused attention It is also the place where employees should be selected because they possess the attributes of patience, personality, and the ability to multi-task.

Why We Mystery Shop

Approximately ten years ago, as a hospital marketing director, Kevin was aware that despite hundreds of thousands of dollars spent each year on advertising, the hospital's market share was eroding. Up to that point, he had attempted to deliver a promise to the community of an organization that was still in line with the core values of the founding Catholic mission. Admittedly, he was attempting to paint a picture of the way the organization wanted to be perceived without really knowing how employees treated customers.

Despite having all sorts of satisfaction data at his disposal, he still couldn't say if employees were pleasant and accommodating at the registration desk, if nurses were respectful of patients, if patients were given eye contact in the ER, or if hospital employees were perceived differently than the competition's. It was assumed that the culture created by the founding order of nuns over a hundred and twenty five years prior was being maintained, but times were changing quickly in healthcare. Did an experience at the hospital genuinely reflect that promise?

Though it was undertaken, customer service training wasn't enough to sustain the promise. The only way to assess the landscape and understand where the organization needed to go was to send in an objective third party to report back with his or her perceptions.

Kevin left the employ of the hospital to offer this primary research resource to hospitals, clinics, and physician practices across the country. While the original intent was to improve frontline customer service, the market has discovered other ways to evaluate processes and services using mystery shopping such as accessibility to physicians, wayfinding, pricing, charity care studies, website and marketing evaluations, and in-depth ways to evaluate the patient experience.

Mystery shopping has also led to an understanding that interpreting primary research cannot in and of itself lead to improved employee behavior, processes, or physical environment. The real value is in solutions to the findings, and that is now Perception Strategies' primary focus.

Tools

Mystery Shop Organizational Claims

Mystery shopping is perhaps the best way to test proposed claims of customer service superiority. After the commitment has been launched internally, mystery shopping can expose pockets of weakness quickly and quietly. It allows you to answer questions such as:

- Can your organization consistently deliver on the promise?
- Are all your customer-contact people on board?
- Does the promise ring true with the customer's perception of the organization?

Role-Play Promises

Role play with employees the use of promises or claims such as new slogans or marketing phrases. Keep in mind that even a phrase like "I'll be with you in just a minute" is seen as a promise by customers. Role-playing allows managers to see their employees in action and gives employees time to feel comfortable with their delivery. It also lets staff discuss how customers perceive certain phrases and slogans. For instance, "I'll be with you in just a minute" is a promise. What does this phrase really mean and how is it interpreted by customers?

Practice Scripted Slogans

Allow employees time to practice using slogans so that they become comfortable using them. For example, one well-known tourist destination answers the telephone, "It's a beautiful day at . . ." to create a pleasant visual for the caller. Make sure that the phrase is not so long and cumbersome that it is difficult to enunciate. If customers cannot understand what is being said because it is done so quickly, it defeats the purpose and confuses the customer.

Chapter 21
Follow Through

> "It was character that got us out of bed, commitment that moved us into action, and discipline that enabled us to follow through."
>
> —Zig Ziglar

Key Levels needed to support the turn on:

   4. Utilize Coaching Techniques
   5. Establish Accountability for Frontline Success

It is a *turn on* when employees do exactly what they say they are going to do, or they surprise customers by doing things they never said they were going to do. Employees who impress customers with their follow through will track down information that is not immediately known. For example, one of these employees would call a customer to say, "I thought you would like to know that the lamp you ordered is being shipped today. I will call you as soon as it arrives in the store."

Arby's Guest Hotline

There is a bumper sticker–like sign at the drive-up windows of the Indianapolis Arby's stores. Below the "Honk if we provided great service" request is a toll-free telephone number customers can call to provide feedback or ask questions.

Kevin wanted to know what happened when people took them up on their offer to ask questions or make comments. So when he called the toll-free number, he expected to talk to someone, but instead got a pleasant message thanking him for calling the Indianapolis Area Arby's Guest Hotline. He was asked to leave a message and then was thanked for taking the time to call. We always like to hear someone thanking us for our time.

Kevin decided to ask a question about something that has been burning on his mind for some time now, namely: What happened to the Arby-Q and was it coming back anytime soon? He also asked if it was possible to get a bunch of Arby-Qs for a party he was having.

The call was made at 9:16 a.m. and a little over 24 hours later he got a call from Gary. Gary first explained that in his 2 1/2 years with Arby's, they hadn't offered the Arby-Q. Many less customer service-minded organizations would have stopped there and, as a customer, Kevin would have accepted that. His contingency plan called for asking how many calls the hotline gets, what kinds of calls they get, and so on.

However, Gary surprised him by saying he talked it over with his boss and that they could make it happen. He asked Kevin how many people were coming to his party to gauge how much meat was going to be required. He then gave Kevin options on how the sandwiches could be packaged for his party. Gary even said they would negotiate a price since they don't offer the sandwich any longer.

Kevin said something silly in his voice mail message about how he could eat a million Arby-Qs. Gary said his boss wanted to take him up on that for a $1 a piece. He said he thought a million dollars would look good on their bottom line. They both laughed.

Why was Kevin turned on? It wasn't that Gary called back. Kevin had had a casual conversation with someone in Arby's management who alluded to the fact that she was scheduled to handle hotline calls, so he knew they took it seriously. It was that they actually discussed the question he had and came up with a customized solution that satisfied him. It was a great customer turn on.

A Volunteer Gets a Letter

During a Perception Strategies customer service training session, a female volunteer who worked at our client's hospital was approached by a manager and handed a letter. The volunteer opened the letter, and since the manager had obviously chosen this moment to present the letter to her, we asked her to share the contents with us. She explained that it was a letter from the hospital's CEO commending her for her actions on behalf of some guests to the hospital.

We asked her to tell us her story since it seemed pertinent to the customer service discussion we were having. She explained that she was at the hospital's front desk when two people in business attire said they were early for a meeting and asked her where they could get a cup of coffee. She gave them directions to the cafeteria.

After about five minutes the two guests returned to the desk. Seeing that they were empty-handed, she realized she had directed them to a closed cafeteria. She was embarrassed. She told them that if they could wait a few minutes she would get them some coffee. She then went to an adjacent department and brewed a fresh pot of coffee for them and returned with two cups.

The guests were so appreciative of her efforts that they personally told the CEO how impressed they were. The volunteer went on to tell us that rather than thinking this was a big deal, she was angry with herself for making the "stupid" mistake of sending them all the way to the cafeteria.

This was a great story to share with the group in the training session because it allowed them to see the impact of truly following through on a customer's request; even when you don't think what you are doing is extraordinary. It also points out that it doesn't take a lot to make a lasting impression.

"Dismissing" Customers

A customer calling for information or help is at the mercy of the employee. When transferred, the result is another instance of uncertainty for the customer. Many customers feel frustration at being transferred without their permission several times during the course of a call.

The typical call transfer situation occurs when the employee doesn't have the information requested and transfers the customer to someone who can help. Take, for example, the following customer, who felt dismissed when an employee transferred her just to get rid of the call. "She said, 'I can transfer you to the business office.' I asked her if they would know the answer and she replied, 'I don't know. Let me transfer you.' Before I could decline to be transferred, she transferred my call.'"

The absence of keeping the customer informed is shown in this observation: "The employee answered the call on the fourth ring. She identified herself as Outpatient Registration. I told her my daughter was going to have a tonsillectomy and wanted to find out about registration. She said, 'Okay, can you hold please?' I said yes, thinking that she would come back on the phone in a moment. Instead, she transferred my call."

This example underscores the message that the employee didn't think enough of the customer's situation to warrant following through on it. Employees often see transferring a call as efficiently getting the caller to the right place. Our mystery shopping research has shown that customers don't always see it that way. Instead, they often perceive it as a breach in the employee's ability to follow through on his or her own.

High-Tech Store Receipts

We encourage organizations to use technology to provide or elicit customer service information. Using store receipts, for instance, is a fantastic idea and a win-win for the customer and the company if the organization is fully prepared to respond when the customer takes them up on it.

The Palmeras Restaurant in the Hilton Caribe Hotel in San Juan makes particularly good use of receipts to improve customer service. At the top of the receipt is an actual survey. On a scale of great, good, regular, and bad, they ask the customer to rate the restaurant in six categories: welcoming, service, food quality, order time, ambiance, and supervisor. To top it off, they have a little room for comments, a phone number, and the restaurant manager's name.

Panera Bread

A client of ours related an experience she had at Panera Bread. She was in a hurry, and the store was mostly vacant. She went to the counter and waited, somewhat impatiently, until someone finally approached her. She asked if they sold gift certificates. They said no but that they did have a new gift card they were just trained on the day before. "In fact," one the employees said, "you will be our first customer."

They began to fiddle with the cash register. "How much would you like it for?" the clerk asked. "Five dollars," our friend said. The two employees were attempting to collectively put their heads together to recall how this was done. They finally got it figured out. One employee said, "Wouldn't it be nice if these came with an envelope?" A manager overheard her and said that they did have envelopes in the back and retrieved one. Then the employee said, "Are you a coffee drinker?" Our client indicated that she was. "Well, let me offer you a free cup of coffee for your trouble, and for being our first gift card customer!" It was not the free coffee that made this experience memorable, it was the fact that they acknowledged that she had waited for them to figure it out.

Tools

Stay with Customers

To avoid the confusion and frustration associated with being bounced from employee to employee, require that employees stay with customers until the encounter's completion. However, if the employee must hand off a customer to another employee, have the employee first explain to the customer why it is in their best interest.

"What do you tell your spouse about work?"

In the absence of direct observation, employees will decide for themselves or be influenced by others into taking a position that is more self-serving and comfortable. This is exacerbated by the fact that many managers are afraid that if they push too hard, employees will quit. Some refuse to observe their employees because they are afraid of their employees or, regrettably, they share the same diminished values. Customer service is not something they are willing to "cause a scene" about unless they are being held accountable.

We often ask employees what they say to their spouse about their boss or employer. Is it, "I just love everybody at work, and those customers, they're the best," or, is it more like, "You can't believe what my boss asked me to do! None of those people at the top have a clue what they're doing. On top of that, I have people asking me the dumbest stuff."

Remember:

- The attitude an employee presents to a loved one is the same underlying attitude they bring to work each day.
- Managers can't control what employees say away from work, but increased observation will make managers more aware of employee attitudes.
- Be aware that there is a connection between an employee's private honesty and the transparency of their poor service delivery to customers.
- Managers can make it clear that negative talk on the job will not be tolerated.

Chapter 22

Employees Showing Pride in Their Work

> "The pride people take in their work transcends to their homes, their education, families and communities."
>
> —Leonard Boswell

Key Levels needed to support the turn on:

1. Communicate a Never-Ending Commitment to Excellence
2. Hire People Who Want to Serve Others
5. Establish Accountability for Frontline Success

Customer service consultant and author Gary Heil says that if an employee doesn't like people—doesn't like talking to people, serving people, or helping people—then that employee ought to find another job. If only it were that easy. We've all seen the signs posted by service organizations begging people to "join our family." Unfortunately, the majority of people taking these jobs do not have the skills or instincts required to provide superior customer service.

When employees have pride in the work they do and truly believe in the quality of the organization, that pride and confidence is evident in every customer interaction. It is also a turn on for customers. The supportive, positive environment created in turn generates satisfaction and loyalty in customers.

Our mystery shopping research has shown that one of the highest qualitative correlations to total customer satisfaction is the perception that employees seem to take pride in what they are doing. The employee's contentment with their present status can be passed on to the customer, creating a relationship of mutual happiness. We are careful to use the word "can" because an employee may be happy with his or her lot in life and not care to pass it on to the customer. Pride in one's job is only relevant if the employee understands that how they treat the customer has a direct effect on the customer's satisfaction.

Do you get the feeling that most employees are proud of their contributions? How can they exude pride in the organization or themselves, for that matter, if they don't really know what it means to be doing what they are doing? How about sending the message, "We hired you because we need you, and we think you're really going to help us." The best way to cultivate employees who care about customers and ultimately contribute to the company's success is to tell them how important they are.

Breckenridge SuperSlide™

Years ago we attended a summer conference in Breckenridge, Colorado. In our free time, we took to the mountains to venture down a commercial attraction known as the SuperSlide™, a Plexiglas slalom run that uses a sled on wheels to take advantage of the snowless mountain. After chairlifting to the top of the ride, we had the choice of two slalom runs: one labeled advanced, and the other labeled beginners. After riding down the beginners run several times, constantly colliding with less adventuresome folks, we noticed that, even though the two runs looked almost identical, things ran much smoother on the advanced course. When we got back to the top, we asked the gentleman responsible for releasing the sleds, "What's the difference between the two runs?" He quickly replied, "Attitude."

That response has stuck with us all these years. Customer service should be viewed in the same way. Employees A and B may look the same, have the same job description, and be hired and trained in the same fashion, but they don't *care* the same. Yet, managers evaluate the two employees in the same way, without consideration for how customers perceive them. The difference between one employee over another is usually his or her attitude toward the customer. If employees are only evaluated on whether or not they could deliver a script, or that customers never said anything negative about their performance, the one factor that separates the winners from the losers is completely missed: *attitude*. How do some employees get the right attitude? They love what they do and take pride in their jobs.

K-Mart

Think about your average week. If you're like most people, you will go grocery shopping, pick up the dry cleaning, go to the movies or rent one, dine out at least once or twice, stop by the local pharmacy, drop by an office supply store, grab a cup of coffee at the neighborhood coffee shop, mail a package or two, and perhaps run to the mall. Certainly you can think of hundreds of additional examples. Have the employees you've interacted with at all those businesses made your life richer through their excellent customer service? We find a good number of these encounters frustrating and upsetting.

On an edition of National Public Radio's "Talk of the Nation," the subject of the show was the announcement that K-Mart was closing almost 300 stores and laying off thousands of employees. They opened up the phone lines to ask Americans for their impressions and what K-Mart has meant to them in their lives.

One caller voiced her opinion that employee attitude and morale contributed to K-Mart's downfall. One doesn't usually hear such comments from the public. We are led to believe by the "experts" that, when something goes amiss, over-capitalization, P/E's, failed mergers, or Martha Stewart had something to do with corporate failures. But here was a woman that the show's screener must have accidentally let slip by because she was suggesting that K-Mart's demise occurred because of a culture in which employees are not proud of where they work and that that translated into poor earnings.

It doesn't take an analyst or consultant to tell you that when you walk through the doors of a K-Mart, you are greeted (or not) by employees who don't seem to want to be there. Or at the very least, by employees who have never learned what it takes to contribute to an environment that enhances the customer's experience.

To be fair, that was the caller's perception, but it has also been ours. Perhaps the employees at K-Mart love what they do, but they have never been taught how to pass that love on to the customer.

A Society of Ungracious Receivers

One of the great challenges that customer service providers face every single day is born out of the fallacy that customers are gracious. Unfortunately, it often seems like the employee-customer relationship is one-sided when it was really meant to be two-way, for example, I help enrich your life by providing this service and you show your appreciation. Instead, those who excel at customer service must learn to ignore the miscreants they are supposed to respect, such as poor tippers and constant complainers.

If customers consistently fail to acknowledge an employee's customer service efforts, assuming the employee met the customers' expectations, then the drive behind those efforts must be pride in one's job, because it certainly isn't customer gratitude. The fact that people can be rude and demanding, and abuse the privilege of being served, is not an excuse—it is an obstacle to be understood and overcome. This is another important reason to cultivate your employees' pride in their work. It will help them weather the rough customers and continue to deliver excellent customer service.

The next fallacy is recognizing and rewarding service excellence. Most service jobs are perceived to be bottom rung. Be the best drive-through server in the history of the 96th Street Wendy's and see where it gets you!

Somehow, we don't envision our sons and daughters cutting their "customer service teeth" as Kevin did as a yard boy at the local yacht club trying to please inebriated boaters, or as a municipal Public Information Officer taking calls from irate citizens wanting their alleys snowplowed. Even so, there are still enough customers who marvel at great service to make it well worth your while. The battle to attain mutual respect between service receivers and providers is one worth fighting.

The Foundry Lesson

In order to help defray the costs of his first year of college, Kevin took a job working in a steel foundry. This particular plant located in Muskegon, Michigan, made engine blocks, among other things, for the automotive industry. It was an incredibly filthy environment. It seemed to take an hour to shower away the day's grit, but the money was great for an 18-year-old kid. It was also an eye-opener to see how workers interacted with one another in this environment.

For three summer months, his primary responsibility was to take the sand mold of an intake valve, dip it into a sludge-like liquid called core wash, and put it through a furnace to bake the wash onto the mold, or core, as it was called. Kevin was never exactly sure why he performed this task. He knew the part he made was assembled with various other parts to create the negative mold of an engine block, which allowed molten steel to find all the spaces where the sand was not present.

Day in and day out Kevin would do the same thing. He was told that if he worked real fast there was the potential to make more money, but he doesn't believe he ever did.

At no time did anyone take him aside to explain how his role fit into the bigger picture. For instance, what are we making, and for whom? There was never the opportunity to look at a new car and think that maybe he had a hand in making it. Perhaps over time he would have picked up on that level of information, but it was clear it was never going to come from his manager. How much time and energy would it have taken for management to explain how Kevin's contribution was important to the organization? You may say, "No one gets that kind of attention!" But if that's true—and we believe it often is—is it any wonder that most of the service employees we encounter each day act as if they don't take any ownership of their work, that they don't have any pride in their jobs?

Most companies have some form of orientation, and it usually satisfies upper management's belief that they have made a contribution to building culture. The problem is that too often management fools themselves into thinking that their words of inspiration have substance. Broad statements and generic aphorisms seldom work. To be informative and motivational, the message must be tailored to the employee's specific role. And unless upper management is willing to speak directly to employees in the "core room," or the cashier at K-Mart, or the clerk at the Bureau of Motor Vehicles, they're unlikely to know how their role fits into the organization they work for. Only a manager can provide that information.

There is certainly a right way and a wrong way for a manager to accomplish this. Back at the steel foundry, a manager telling Kevin that, "Unless this intake valve is dipped with the right amount of wash on it, we can't use the piece and that's going to cost the company money" would have been taking a negative approach. While this approach can scare an employee into performing well, it is unlikely to build long-term satisfaction and pride in his work. A more positive message would be, "You may not realize it, but that intake valve you are working on is critical to the engine that is going into every 1975 Chrysler LeBaron. In fact, we are going to be producing 25 percent of all the engine blocks going into Chrysler cars for the new model year. So every time you see a new Cordoba, Imperial, or Newport, there is a good chance you helped put that car on the road."

Tools

"Act as if you own the place."

Futurist Clay Sherman struck a chord at a conference Kevin attended recently. He implored attendees to go back to their respective jobs and "act as if you own the place." Only through pride in one's job can an employee convey a sense of ownership. Every employee should be encouraged to approach customer service in that way. Managers can do that by reminding employees of how valuable their contribution is and praising and reinforcing positive behavior.

Building an Awards Program

Awards that recognize, validate, and value exceptional work keep employees motivated, productive, and efficient. They are an effective way to reinforce good employee behavior, as well as the company's expectations and goals. An awards program makes employees feel that they are a valuable asset to the company, and that they actually make a difference. An employee that feels appreciated at work is more likely to have a higher job satisfaction rate. A higher job satisfaction rate leads to a higher employee retention rate.

1. *Different levels of an awards program.*

There are different levels in an awards program that reward an employee according to the degree of exceptional work they display. It is up to the company to determine what type of work falls in to each of the categories: small, medium, and large. It should require additional exceptional work to reach each level, and the rewards should increase with each level.

- **Level One** should be obtainable by all employees who adhere to the company's policies and display exceptional employee behavior. The rewards for this level should be small; for example, gift certificates, written notes of thanks, and paper awards.
- **Level Two** should be obtainable by going above and beyond what is expected by the company. This level should be reserved for employees who demonstrate that their ability is above and beyond the norm. The rewards for this level should be medium; for example, a longer lunch break, small amount of time off, or a commemorative plaque.

- **Level Three** should not be attainable by every employee. This level should be reserved for the employee who has demonstrated exceptional behavior on a repetitive basis. The employee should have already received, at least, one level-one and one level-two awards. The rewards for this level should be large; for example, acknowledgment by the CEO, CFO, and so on, a ceremony held in their honor, or a larger amount of paid time off.

2. ***Each level of the awards program must be special.***

There are five keys to employee recognition that ensure your employee will feel valued and honored. These five keys are human interaction, peer recognition, receiving a useful and functional award, family involvement, and immediate gratification. Not all of these keys must be met in each level, but the closer you get, the more gratifying it is for the employee.

- **Human Interaction**—The award should not mysteriously appear on the employee's desk. There must be interaction between the employer and the employee to ensure recognition.
- **Peer Recognition**—The award should not be secretly given; to boost employee morale and make the employee feel special, the award should be acknowledged to all peers.
- **A Useful and Functional Award**—The award should not be a piece of computer paper that can be bent, thrown away, or will get yucky quickly. It should be something useful and functional, such as a new nametag with the award inscribed on it, a paperweight with the award inscribed, a gift certificate, a day off, and so on. The more useful and functional the award, the more valuable it is and the harder the employees strive to achieve it.
- **Family Involvement**—Whenever possible the family should be involved in the award. Invite the family to the ceremony, give a gift certificate that the entire family can use, or simply send a card to the employee's home to notify the family on their achievement.

- **Immediate Gratification**—The employee should get his or her award in a timely manner. In other words, the employee should not be rewarded six months after the desired behavior. By rewarding desired behavior immediately the employee is more likely to continue the behavior, and others are more likely to follow.

Chapter 23
Going the Extra Mile

"There are no traffic jams along the extra mile."

—Roger Staubach

Key Levels needed to support the turn on:

1. Communicate a Never-Ending Commitment to Excellence
2. Hire People Who Want to Serve Others
3. Directly and Routinely Observe Employees in Action
4. Utilize Coaching Techniques
5. Establish Accountability for Frontline Success
6. Reward Those Who Excel in Customer Service

The phrase "going the extra mile" has always signified a willingness to do whatever it takes for customers. Is it any wonder it *turns* them *on*? This highest form of customer service causes customers to say to others, "You're not going to believe what they did!"

Management often assumes that their people will behave in a consistent, professional manner and occasionally go the extra mile because it is the commonsense thing to do. But employees fail to respond to opportunities to go the extra mile because no one ever told them that it was okay to step out of the box, or they are led to believe by management that taking matters into their own hands is a rules violation. In addition, employees may be stalled in an unsupportive culture, receiving a lack of management direction, going unrecognized for their efforts, or be unequipped to understand consumer need and motivation.

The following is an example from a Perception Strategies mystery shop that shows a focused healthcare employee genuinely caring for the welfare of her customer:

"Jan went above and beyond the standard for good customer service. As we were concluding the conversation, she gave me very helpful information about areas of town to avoid living in due to high fumes, as she did not want my daughter's asthma to be affected. She even offered to help find a daycare for my daughter that was trained with breathing treatments. She was genuine and compassionate. Her extra effort leaves no room for improvement and her overall customer service skills are excellent."

Jan, the employee, did two things she did not have to do. She provided information about parts of town that would be unhealthy for the customer's asthmatic daughter, and she offered to help locate a suitable daycare. If she does neither of these, she will likely be perceived as just a nice employee doing her job. It is the unexpectedness of her actions, and their obvious and immediate value to the customer, that drives the positive overall perception.

The extra mile is achieved most easily when employees know what will delight customers even before customers do. Work with your employees to determine where opportunities exist and what they should be willing to do for customers. In order to open employees up to extra mile opportunities, pose this question: "If you got the chance, what would be a way for you to go the extra mile for the customer?" Allow them to use their imagination as they explore what it takes to stretch their boundaries. This exercise will also let employees know they are supported in their ideas. Hopefully, they will be encouraged to come up with examples such as:

- Making a personal delivery to a customer
- Offering to connect the customer with another vendor
- Staying late to help a customer
- Coming into work on a day off to help a customer

Another effective strategy for motivating employees to go the extra mile is to create a series of if/then scenarios. For instance, you might ask your staff, "If you were to provide information without being asked, what would the customer's response be?" Let them see the cause and effect of certain actions.

Hopefully they will come to the realization that, in this particular example, the customer appreciates that the employee has unexpectedly helped him or her make a more informed decision. Another kind of if/then scenario is one in which managers pose a set of customer problems/issues to the employees and ask what the employee might do to help.

Going the extra mile is a fluid proposition that constantly needs fine-tuning. Thomas Connellan and Ron Zempke write in *Sustaining Knock Your Socks Off Service*, "Sustaining high quality service is the result of keeping focused on changing customer expectations and continually modifying internal processes to maintain a leadership position." To be sure, the constant pursuit of customer service excellence is a "what have you done for me lately?" proposition. Every employee becomes measured against the one employee who was willing to perform the extraordinary. And yet, with every additional effort to go the extra mile, an organization quickly distances itself from the competition.

R-E-P-E-A-T Performance

Efforts to go the extra mile cannot go unnoticed or they will fade. Employees must be made aware that the effort they make on behalf of customers is critically important to the organization. R-E-P-E-A-T Performance is a recognition program that focuses employees on the fact that going the extra mile is the ultimate display of customer respect and appreciation.

The six R-E-P-E-A-T Performance steps support the creation and maintenance of a Going the Extra Mile employee recognition award program:

Reinforce Behavior

Take the following actions to reinforce an exceptional service experience:

- Interview the employee to understand what he or she was thinking or trying to accomplish that resulted in the customer's response.
- Read the details of the experience to the staff pointing out the specific behavior or actions taken by the recipient.
- Praise the employee in front of his/her peers and encourage the rest of the staff to take similar actions.

Educate

Customer service training and new employee orientation should include:

- A portion on what it means to go the extra mile and how employees are recognized for these efforts.
- Role-playing and real "stories" to demonstrate the organization's desire to have this become the norm.
- Affirmative satisfaction survey comments and letters sent to management.

Promote

Develop a campaign in your organization creating awareness for the award program:

- Utilize all available mediums within your organization to communicate the award experience and to reinforce the fact that opportunities to exceed customer expectations can be simple, quick, and rewarding.
- Communicate this through emails, memos, bulletin boards, newsletters, department meetings, or the intranet.

Expose

To further expose those who are exceeding expectations, employees should be encouraged to recognize each other for going above and beyond for customers by writing a note or letter to the department head or CEO sharing the outstanding customer service acts of their fellow employee.

Care should be taken, however, to discourage recognition that is not customer-focused. An employee may want to offer praise for something that another employee did for them. While this may be fine for another program, the intent of the award is to shine the light on those who understand how essential it is to be "pro-customer."

Award

Create a "Going the Extra Mile" recognition awards program. Employees acknowledged for their efforts could receive recognition in addition to the aforementioned praise in front of their peers. Different types of awards recognize customer service excellence: formal and informal.

Examples of informal awards are:

- Extended lunch hours
- Movie passes
- Sporting, musical, or cultural event tickets
- Retail gift cards

Examples of formal awards might be:

- A letter of recognition signed by the CEO
- A formal certificate of acknowledgment recognizing the employee for going above and beyond
- A lapel pin to recognize award nominees
- A generous prize to the year-end award winner

We suggest creating special times to distribute the awards. Emphasize the achievement in order to promote the goal of customer service excellence. This can be done during a monthly meeting, on Employee

Recognition Day, or at an end of the year banquet. The more often the organization recognizes excellence in the workplace, the better.

If the department has monthly meetings, be certain to dedicate at least five minutes of the monthly meeting toward recognizing an employee and allow a few minutes for the recognized employee to share with their co-workers tips of their success.

An Employee Recognition Day can be a picnic or a luncheon where employees are recognized for their dedication to their customers. End of the year banquets are an excellent time to make formal recognition truly grand by awarding an outstanding Extra Mile Award winner. The award should be presented by the Chief Executive Officer of the organization.

Train Again

As with any initiative, it is important to keep it going. Repeat the training process to take advantage of previous successes. This will add to the numbers of employees who are exceeding customer expectations and continue to strengthen the organization's resolve to put the customer first. Over time, the organization will experience a shift from self-centered behavior to customer-centered behavior as employees achieve greater satisfaction in helping others.

Rewarding "Extra Mile" Effort

At Perception Strategies, part of the service we provide is to have our mystery shoppers identify employees who go the extra mile. Not surprisingly, it is called The Extra Mile Award. We believe that customer service research is as much about finding people doing things right as it is about finding inconsistency. We provide the employee's manager with a certificate that they can present to the employee. In the body of the certificate we include the positive comments made by the mystery shoppers. Our goal is not only to recognize employee excellence, but to also heighten awareness of how good it can feel to be praised by customers.

Recognition for customer service excellence should be a comprehensive effort to reward outstanding employees and motivate others to emulate their actions. When an employee is recognized for exceptional service, they feel proud of their contribution to the organization, and this positive reinforcement leads to more committed employees and loyal customers.

Employees who have customer service as part of their job responsibilities are often thought to be "simply doing their job." However, "doing your job" is an organizational expectation. Recognizing exceptional service is about *customer* expectations. If employees are enthusiastic or provide more assistance than was anticipated, they have gone far beyond what customers have come to expect from any customer service provider.

If an organization did nothing other than study positive customer feedback to understand why they respond the way they do, enough information would be available to create the kind of service environment all organizations should be striving to achieve.

Anatomy of an Incredible Call

Going the extra mile can be achieved by doing one big thing for a customer, but it can also be a series of little things that when accumulated overwhelm customers. Such is the case with the following example of a physician referral customer service representative.

We often use the following mystery shopping experience as an aid in training call center employees because it exemplifies a customer service representative (CSR) who consciously "handles" the caller with the intent of creating an extra mile experience.

Credit must go to the managers of this call center because much of what the CSR does she was trained to do, such as the core elements of identification, how to provide referral information, and direct the caller to the website. However, the style and extra effort used by the CSR to gain the confidence of the caller is all her own.

The call was answered on the first ring by Jennifer. She immediately identified the department and herself. Jennifer then asked, "May I help you?" The caller said, "Yes, my doctor recently diagnosed me with arthritis. He recommended seeing a rheumatologist. Can you give me the names of some specialists?" "Sure," Jennifer said in an upbeat tone, "but first I need some information for my database." *It's only one word, but "sure" immediately sent the message to the caller that help was imminent. It was also a great segue into a request for information.*

After the caller gave her name, Jennifer asked for the spelling of her name. This request symbolized to the customer a desire to be accurate and respectful of the person's identity. From that point on, Jennifer addressed the caller by name.

Jennifer asked the caller, "Is your doctor from our hospital?" She was told that she was not. She then asked the caller how she heard about the referral service. She was told that a friend had told her about the service. *Jennifer expressed her appreciation for the referral by asking the caller to thank her friend for the recommendation, which was a very imaginative follow-up to the referral inquiry.*

Jennifer continued by asking the caller if she preferred a male or female doctor and what insurance will be used. Jennifer said, "There are three doctors that come up. Do you have a pen and paper?" *This question communicated to the customer that the CSR was only going to start when the customer was ready.*

The caller said, "Just a minute, there never seems to be a pen when you need it." Jennifer responded with, "You must live at my house, I have the same problem." *Regardless of how trivial it may seem, customers enjoy a personal reference.*

Jennifer said, "I can send you a list of the doctors after our call so you will have them." The caller said, "That's okay, I found a pen—you can just give me the doctors' names." *Offering to send a list of doctors was just another added service that went above and beyond.*

Jennifer gave the name, location, and room number of the first doctor. She followed that up with the telephone number. Jennifer then told the caller all of the doctor's credentials, including age, schooling, how long she has been practicing medicine, board certifications, and teaching affiliation to the hospital.

Jennifer gave the same information for the second doctor including spelling out the doctor's name. When she provided the doctor's office location, she asked the caller, "Do you know where that is?" *This exemplified Jennifer's desire to constantly make sure there were no missing gaps in the customer's understanding.*

Jennifer provided a similarly thorough review on the third doctor. The caller then asked, "What are the doctor's hours?" Jennifer said, "I have no hours listed, but when I have tried to set up appointments for patients, the doctors seem to have business hours like eight to five." *This is a key point in the encounter. Customers often appreciate it when service providers offer information based on experience even if they acknowledge that the exact information is not readily available.*

Jennifer said, "If it were not Saturday, I would try to set up an appointment for you." *This statement said to the customer that Jennifer was willing to do even more if it were possible.*

Jennifer asked, "Do you have access to the web?" When the caller said she did, Jennifer directed her to the web address, sharing that it provided information on physicians in addition to their photos. "Some people feel more comfortable when they see what the doctor looks like," she said. *She could have easily stopped when she provided the web address, but instead explained what was contained in the site.*

Jennifer then added additional value, "You can call your doctor to find out if he is familiar with any of the doctors I gave you." She asked if she could help the caller with anything else, thanked her for calling, and said goodbye.

As a result of this overwhelmingly positive experience, the caller observed that Jennifer truly cared about her. She also suggested that if there were awards for employee of the week or month, the caller would vote for Jennifer. This experience also illustrates what is possible when a service provider is willing to ensure that the customer is totally cared for every step of the way.

Tools

Implementing R-E-P-E-A-T Performance

The key to rolling out a recognition program is to continuously keep the focus on customer perception and satisfaction. The following are some of the ideas for launching the program:

- Create a teaser program to introduce employee meetings. Use a slogan such as the Roger Staubach quote that opens this chapter, "There are no traffic jams along the extra mile." Invite employees to come to a meeting to find out how they can get on the fast track to personal rewards.
- Roll out the program at employee meetings.
- Use dramatizations to show the difference between unacceptable, acceptable, and extra mile efforts.
- Show examples of each R-E-P-E-A-T step.

Index

A
abdication, 22
accountability, xvii–xviii, 54
acknowledgment, customer service, 12, 88–89
apologies, 29, 127
assessment of rules, 29
attention seekers (employees), 38–40
attitude, 44–45, 186–187
awards programs (employees), 191–193, 197, 200–201

B
barriers to customer service, 21
bending the rules, 27–29
Bossidy, Larry, 18

C
Charan, Ram, 18
coaching techniques, xvii, 45–46
communication, xv
competition, 119
confrontational situations, 123–124
consistency, 145–154
corporate culture, 3–5
corporate mandates, 26–27
counter barriers, 21
creativity, employees, 55–59
cross-departmental staff meetings, 67
cross-selling, 112–114
culture
    corporate culture, 3–5
    creativity, 55–59
    friendliness, 85
The Customer Comes Second, 142
Customer Service Acting 101, 78–79
customers
    acknowledgment, 12, 88–89
    confrontational situations, 123–124
    customer service
        "Determined to Delight" initiative, 19–20
        job security, 11
        making it all about the customer, 1–13
        perception of transactions, 78–79
        versus selling, 110–111, 118
    feedback, 104

managing difficult customers, 75–76
reading, 134–135
six levels to service excellence, xiv–xviii
   accountability, xvii–xviii
   communicating commitment to excellence, xv
   direct observation of employees, xvi
   employee rewards, xviii
   selective hiring practices, xv–xvi
   utilization of coaching techniques, xvii
tolerance of, 128
turn ons, xviii–xi
   consistency, 145–154
   customer recognition, 93–99
   delivering on promises, 169–177
   employee creativity, 55–59
   employees showing pride in their work, 185–193
   employees who like to serve, 37–46
   empowered employees, 137–143
   engaging the customer, 47–54
   follow through, 179–184
   friendliness, 77–85
   Going the Extra Mile, 195–204
   helping customers make decisions, 109–119
   knowledgeable employees, 31–36
   making it all about the customer, 1–13
   matching customer's pace, 87–91
   no preconceived notions, 129–135
   no rules, 25–29
   proactivity, 101–108
   relinquishing power to the customer, 15–23
   respect, 69–76
   responsiveness, 155–167
   taking the high road, 121–128
   teamwork, 61–67

D

decision-making, 109–119
delivering on promises, 169–177
"Determined to Delight" customer service initiative, 19–20
direct observation of employees, xvi, 42–43, 51–53
dismissal of customers, 181–182

E

education of employees, 117, 198
employees
   accountability, 54
   awards programs, 191–193
   compliments, 66
   creativity, 55–59
   education of, 117, 198
   empowerment, 137–143
   exposure, 199
   frontline, 29
   knowledgeable employees, 31–36
   mandated friendliness, 79–81
   motivators. *See* turn ons
   mutual proactivity, 102–103
   negativism, 66
   pride in their work, 185–193

promotion, 198
R-E-P-E-A-T Performance recognition program, 197
respect for the organization, 127–128
rewards, xviii
service employees, 37–46
training, 200
engaging the customer, 47–54
Execution-The Discipline of Getting Things Done, 18
exposure of employees, 199
eye contact, 53

F

Family Involvement award (employees), 192
feedback, 104
follow through, 179–184
friendliness, 77–85
frontline employees, 29
frontline training, 6–7

G

glass partition barriers, 21
Going the Extra Mile, 195–204

H

helping customers make decisions, 109–119
hiring practices, xv-xvi, 40–41
Human Interaction award (employees), 192

I

"I'm done when you say I'm done" mantra, 9–10
"I'm ready when you are" mantra, 7–8
identification of customer's pace, 90
Immediate Gratification award (employees), 193
inanimate objects (employees), 38–40
insider terms, 23
invisible customers, 73–74

J

job security, customer service, 11
"just a second" rule, 8

K

Keep the Customer board game, 106
kindnesses, 85
knowledgeable employees, 31–36

L

line of sight, 5–6
little kindnesses, 85

M

magical mission statement, 171–172
managers
    difficult customers, 75–76
    leading by example, 143
mandates, 79-81, 114–116
mantras, 7-10
matching customer's pace, 77–85

mission (organizational journey), 141–142, 171–172
motivators (employees). *See* turn ons
mystery shopping, 176
mythical origins of bad service, 146

O

observation of employees, xvi, 42-43, 51–53
outside-in perception exercise, 125–126

P

Peer Recognition award (employees), 192
perception
    customer service transactions, 78–79
    outside-in exercise, 125–126
preconceived notions, 129–135
proactivity, 101–108
product knowledge, education of employees, 117
promises, delivering on, 167–177
promotion of employees, 198

R

R-E-P-E-A-T Performance recognition program, 197
reading customers, 134–135
recognition
    customer recognition, 93–99
    R-E-P-E-A-T Performance program, 197
recovering business, 138–140
reinforcement of behavior, 198

relinquishing power to the customer, 15–23
respect, 69–76, 127–128
responsiveness, 155–167
rewards, xviii
role-playing promises, 177
rules
    assessment of, 29
    bending the rules, 27–29
    "just a second," 8
    no rules customer turn on, 25–29

S

saboteurs (employees), 38–40
scripted slogans, 177
scripts, 51, 71
selective hiring practices, xv–xvi
selling *versus* customer service, 110–111, 118
selling/cross-selling opportunities, 36
service delays, 91
service employees, 37–46
service shticks, 57–59
shticks (service shticks), 57–59
six levels to customer service excellence, xiv–xviii
    accountability, xvii–xviii
    communicating commitment to excellence, xv
    direct observation of employees, xvi
    employee rewards, xviii
    selective hiring practices, xv–xvi
    utilization of coaching techniques, xvii
slogans, 177

STAR AWARD (BMV), 17–18

T

taking the high road, 121–128
teamwork, 61–67
telephone encounters, 74–75, 119
tolerance of customers, 128
tools
    assisting customers to make decisions, 117–119
    avoiding preconceived notions, 134–135
    consistency, 153–154
    customer recognition, 98–99
    delivering on promises, 176–177
    developing knowledgeable employees, 36
    employees showing pride in their work, 190–193
    empowered employees, 142–143
    engaging the customer, 53–54
    follow through, 183–184
    fostering employee creativity, 59
    friendliness, 85
    hiring employees who like to serve, 45–46
    implementation of R-E-P-E-A-T performance recognition program, 204
    making it all about the customer, 12–13
    matching customer's pace, 90–91
    no rules customer turn on, 29
    proactivity, 107–108
    relinquishing power to the customer, 22–23

    respect, 75–76
    responsiveness, 166–167
    taking the high road, 127–128
    teamwork, 66–67
training
    employees, 200
    frontline, 6–7
turn ons (customers), xviii–xi
    consistency, 145–154
    customer recognition, 93–99
    delivering on promises, 169–177
    employee creativity, 55–59
    employees showing pride in their work, 185–193
    employees who like to serve, 37–46
    empowered employees, 137–143
    engaging the customer, 47–54
    follow through, 179–184
    friendliness, 77–85
    Going the Extra Mile, 195–204
    helping customers make decisions, 109–119
    knowledgeable employees, 31–36
    making it all about the customer, 1–13
    matching customer's pace, 87–91
    no preconceived notions, 129–135
    no rules, 25–29
    proactivity, 101–108
    relinquishing power to the customer, 15–23
    respect, 69–76
    responsiveness, 155–167
    taking the high road, 121–128
    teamwork, 61–67

U

unique service shticks, 57–59
Useful and Functional award (employees), 192
utilization of coaching techniques, xvii

W

waves of attitude, 44–45
"word of mouth is too slow" theory, 34–35

Printed in the United States
59423LVS00002B/40-90